IMAGES
of America

HISTORIC MONTE NE

William Hope "Coin" Harvey (1851–1936) was the founder and driving force behind the Monte Ne resort. His history included serving as a teacher, lawyer, silver mine owner, real estate developer, promoter, publisher, author, debater, lecturer, campaigner, resort developer, good roads booster, doomsayer, and presidential candidate. (Courtesy of RHM.)

ON THE COVER: What attracted folks like these to Monte Ne? While the cold spring water and amenities such as boating, fishing, and fine hotels were enjoyable, the social experience of visiting with family and friends and meeting others was a big draw. (Courtesy of RHM.)

IMAGES
of America

HISTORIC MONTE NE

Allyn Lord
Rogers Historical Museum

ARCADIA
PUBLISHING

ISBN 978-0-7385-4336-9

Published by Arcadia Publishing
Charleston, South Carolina

Printed in the United States of America

Library of Congress Catalog Card Number: 2006928105

For all general information contact Arcadia Publishing at:
Telephone 843-853-2070
Fax 843-853-0044
E-mail sales@arcadiapublishing.com
For customer service and orders:
Toll-Free 1-888-313-2665

Visit us on the Internet at www.arcadiapublishing.com

Although "Coin" Harvey is often portrayed as the star of historic Monte Ne, this book is dedicated to all the people who have lived and worked in Silver Springs and Monte Ne over the past century and a half. Their stories and their lives have enriched the history of Northwest Arkansas.

Contents

ACKNOWLEDGMENTS

The story of Monte Ne covers more than a century and recounts the lives of thousands, both past and present. It is impossible to acknowledge everyone whose work or life story has blessed this book, but I humbly thank each of you.

At the Rogers Historical Museum (RHM), director Gaye Bland provided support, scanning, and technical assistance; and curator of collections Sarah Price helped track down collections and scanned images. I offer them my heartfelt thanks. My great appreciation goes to staff at the Shiloh Museum of Ozark History (SMOH): photo archivist Marie Demeroukas tracked down information, scanned many images, and proofread; collections staff Carolyn Reno and Heather Marie Wells helped find Monte Ne collections; and Susan Young provided support and technical expertise.

My unending gratitude goes to Trude Swift and Betty Mullenix, who for several years volunteered their time to pour through microfilm of Rogers newspapers. Another volunteer, Jeannette Walker, transcribed all the Harvey family letters in the museum collections. These three were the research backbone of the project and will no doubt have a special place in heaven.

Thanks to those who graciously allowed me to use their images: Karen Armstrong, the Benton County Historical Society, Bob Besom, Donna Charlesworth, Howard Clark, Addie L. Colclasure, Thelma Graham, Eva Graves, Duane Hand, Herbert Holcomb, Lorene Huckstep, Nan Lawler, Kay Lockwood, David Purdy, Don Roemer, the Saunders Memorial Museum, Ada Lee Shook, Jim Skipper, the *Springdale News*, Betty Swearingen, Paula Thompson, Mrs. Kenneth Tillotson, Marion Warner, the Washington County Historical Society, and Robert Winn. My appreciation goes to those who helped answer questions or track down bits of information, including Jim Barrack, Opal Beck, the late Kenneth Doescher, Tom Duggan, Charles Harvey, Mary Sue Hewgley, Mandy Hougland, Gene Hull, Jan Lancaster, Jim McWhorter, and Stephen Mitten. I also thank editor Adam Ferrell at Arcadia Publishing, who was always available for advice and consultation.

Last but not least, I'm incredibly grateful to my family and friends who've supported me in this work and in all my life's journeys. And love and kisses to the Boys.

INTRODUCTION

The story of Monte Ne is rich and textured and spans more than a century, from its predecessor Silver Springs to the lively community of Monte Ne today. And while there are many individual stories to be told about both Silver Springs and today's Monte Ne, the story of historic Monte Ne is inextricably linked to the story of William Coin Harvey.

William Hope Harvey was born on August 16, 1851, on a farm near Buffalo in what was then Virginia (now West Virginia). He was the fifth of six children born to Anna Marie DaLimbroux Hope, a strong Episcopalian whose lineage can be traced back to Virginia, and Robert Trigg Harvey, a Scotts-Irish farmer and one-time member of the Virginia legislature. During the Civil War, Billy, as he was then called, and his family moved to a farm and the boys attended class in a log schoolhouse. When Harvey was about 14, he went to the Buffalo Academy, and at age 16, he was sufficiently educated to teach a three-month term of grade school. After a semester at Marshall College in nearby Guyandotte, Virginia, Harvey taught one more term.

Following in the footsteps of older brother Thomas, Harvey then decided to study law and was admitted to the West Virginia Bar at age 19. He joined Thomas as a law partner in Huntington, West Virginia, and designed his own home there, a house which still stands and is notable for its early use of cement stucco.

In 1875, Harvey moved to Gallipolis, Ohio, where he met Anna Halliday, four years his junior and the daughter of wholesaler John T. Halliday and his wife, Mary. They married a year later and made the first of the many moves that would eventually take them to six states. Daughter Marie Hope and son Robert Halliday ("Hal") were born in Cleveland. The family then moved to Chicago in 1879 where Harvey practiced law and became the attorney for millionaire banker Amos J. Snell, which many believe contributed to Harvey's lifelong distrust of the effects of great wealth.

Settling back in Gallipolis, Harvey became an attorney for wholesale houses. Son Thomas William was born there in 1882. On a business trip for a client in 1883, Harvey stopped in Colorado. He then decided to move the family to the southwest part of that state to invest in silver mining and real estate, due, he said, "to my health being impaired by overwork in the practice of law." With his family and 10 laborers, he took over operation of the Silver Bell, one of the best-producing silver mines in the state, which was located just north of Ouray. Daughter Annette was born there in 1885. It may have been the many resorts in the Ouray area in the 1870s and 1880s that first drew Harvey's attention to the resort business.

In 1887, mining costs increased, and the price of silver began to plummet. A year later, Harvey abandoned the mine, with no profit, and moved his family to Pueblo, Colorado. There he practiced law, took up real estate development, and became one of the major developers of Pueblo's Mineral Palace, an ornate exposition hall promoting Colorado's mining resources. The project was so successful that Gov. Job Cooper bestowed on him the rank of colonel in the state militia, a title that stuck with Harvey through his days at Monte Ne.

Despite the honor, Harvey left Pueblo in 1891, apparently without paying his $5,000 pledge to the project. He moved his family briefly to Denver and then to Ogden, Utah, where he promoted an extravagant Mardi Gras–like carnival called the "Order of Monte Cristo." The carnival was a popular success but also a financial failure.

In the 1870s and 1880s, there was a contentious debate about whether a gold-only-based currency ("monometallism") or a gold-and-silver-based currency ("bimetallism") was the better American financial system, and it was about to draw Harvey into the brawl. After the repeal of the Silver Purchase Act, restoring gold as the sole currency standard, a money panic and crash in June 1893 sent the economy into a deep depression. In the West, the silver collapse led to massive unemployment and a crash in the real estate market. With yet another financial failure and the serious economic problems facing the nation, author Jeannette Nichols noted that Harvey "had come to feel an antipathy for gold monometallism." He decided to return to Chicago to promote the cause of bimetallism. This was the family's seventh move in 17 years.

Harvey started the Coin Publishing Company, devoted to preaching against the monopoly of gold and for the free coinage of silver at a ratio to gold of 16 to 1. In December 1893, Harvey began a quarterly series of short paperback books called *Coin's Financial Series* and wrote six of the nine books in that series himself. The most popular one, *Coin's Financial School*, told of a 10-year-old boy, Coin, who taught an economics class on the monetary debate. While Coin was supposedly fictional, the adult audience members were given the names of real-life "goldbugs" (those supporting the gold standard) and were made to seem foolish and to lack Coin's intelligence and critical thinking. By the end of class, his audience was won over to bimetallism. The book had an accessible style for the masses, and few failed to recognize that Coin was really Harvey himself. Harvey thereafter was known by that nickname. *Coin's Financial School* was published in June 1894, and its circulation eventually reached several million copies, becoming one of the top best sellers of the 19th century. It even spawned a rash of books in counterargument, including everything from serious refutations to parodies and ridicule. More importantly, the book's success sent Harvey on the road around the country, engaging in successful, standing-room-only debates with goldbugs in 1895.

As the presidential election year drew close, Harvey felt that members from any party who believed in the free-silver argument should unite on a single ticket. He got on the bandwagon of William Jennings Bryan, however, a magnificent orator who delivered at the 1896 Democratic convention his now-famous "Cross of Gold" speech. Bryan criticized the gold standard and advocated inflating the currency by the free coinage of silver, and some have suggested that Harvey actually was the ghostwriter for that speech. Bryan went on to win the Democratic presidential nomination. Harvey fully backed Bryan and stumped for him around the country. In his later years, Harvey described himself as Bryan's advisor and close friend.

Bryan lost the presidential race to William McKinley. In 1898, the chair of the Democratic National Committee, Sen. James Kimbrough Jones of Arkansas, appointed Harvey chair of the ways and means committee (which dealt with taxation, tariffs, and some entitlement programs). In late fall 1899, however, Harvey resigned the chair after the National Committee decided to abandon the money subject.

Disgusted with national politics and the abandonment of the free-silver issue, Harvey once again found a new challenge and re-created himself. While campaigning for Bryan in 1896, Harvey had visited Northwest Arkansas and found it reminiscent of his home state of West Virginia. And so it was to Arkansas that author, debater, and silverite Coin Harvey retreated in 1899.

One

Silver Springs

About five miles southeast of Rogers, the 400-acre community of Silver Springs found its home in a lush valley through which ran the Silver Springs branch of Spring Creek, a feeder to the White River. Silver Springs was fed by 12 springs with a year-round water temperature of 51 degrees Fahrenheit. The largest, Big Spring, ran at 10,000 gallons per minute. The other springs included Elixir, Lithia, Spout, Seven Sisters, and Blowing, all situated among the elms, oaks, and sycamores of the valley. (Courtesy of RHM.)

A three-story gristmill was built in 1857 after the half-mile Silver Springs Creek was channeled into a waterfall to run the mill's overshot wheel. The area had long been known as one of the beauty spots of the region, and the mill frequently served as a gathering place for farmers and picnickers. During the Civil War, the mill changed hands numerous times and helped provide flour for troops from both the North and South. The earliest-known mill owners were James R. Pettigrew in the 1880s and Daniel Portnell from 1889 to 1895. Portnell sold his interest in the mill to Rev. J. G. Bailey, a former pastor of the Rogers Congregational Church. It was Bailey who sold his 320 acres at Silver Springs to Coin Harvey in May 1900. (Courtesy of RHM.)

A distillery built about one-half mile downstream from the Silver Springs mill was operated in the 1830s by Abe McGarrah and his brother-in-law and output 30 gallons a day. This tavern, built in 1856 or 1857, no doubt served the many farmers and visitors to Silver Springs. (Courtesy of RHM.)

As is true of the road to Monte Ne today, the road to Silver Springs from the Rogers area was steep and winding. Its ruggedness, however, failed to deter hundreds of visitors to the area's coolness, including Leon Powell, seen here in 1913. (Courtesy of SMOH/Betty Swearingen.)

The number of visitors to Silver Springs increased in the late 1800s with the addition of a two-story, frame auditorium, which hosted local bands, speakers, and performers. Its location is uncertain, but clearly it must have been near the creek, given the johnboat at bottom right. (Courtesy of RHM.)

By the 1890s, Silver Springs consisted of a store, post office, auditorium, and mill, along with numerous homes and farms. Visitors found cool temperatures, good fishing and hunting, and a chance to socialize. It is no surprise that the area was perceived by Coin Harvey as "distinctly charming." (Courtesy of RHM.)

Two

THE BIRTH OF MONTE NE

William Coin Harvey (here about 1900) purchased a small acreage in Silver Springs in 1899. He returned from Chicago in May 1900 and, being well known for *Coin's Financial School* and his free-silver debates, lectured in Rogers on the free-silver issue. In October, he purchased Reverend Bailey's 320 acres in Silver Springs for $3,229. From that point on, Harvey made the area his home. "The people of Arkansas," Harvey wrote, "are to be congratulated on having no large city and no extremely rich people. For these reasons I have come here to make my home." (Courtesy of SMOH/Washington County Historical Society.)

While Harvey rarely advertised the area as a health resort, friend W. T. McWhorter later said Harvey "saw the chance to develop a watering place in the Ozarks where people could boil out the poisonous effects of voting the Republican ticket and defending the gold standard." (Courtesy of SMOH.)

The postmaster had wanted to change the town's name due to confusion in mail delivery with Siloam Springs. Harvey's land purchase made a name change timely. He thought Monte Ne (purportedly a combination of the Spanish and Omaha Indian words for "mountain water") "fits the tongue attractively." (Courtesy of SMOH.)

Harvey wrote in 1902 that he was familiar with American and European resorts but that he felt Monte Ne was unique. It had something "so distinctly charming in the evidences of nature's handiwork at this spot that [I] believed others could not but be similarly impressed." Caves such as this one (top) and tall limestone cliffs such as Eagles' Nest (bottom) were common but beautiful sights around the White River and Monte Ne valley. (Courtesy of RHM.)

Harvey first went to work on Monte Ne's waterways. He hired Albert Graham of Lowell to supervise the dredging of a canal. He built masonry abutments to form a floodgate, which narrowed Silver Springs Creek between Big Spring and Elixir Spring, creating Big Spring Lake. Graham then channeled most of the rest of the creek to form what Harvey called the lagoon. He believed that "the wonderful clearness and freshness of this water excites instant comment." The *Rogers Democrat* declared, "The lake at the big spring has been filled, making a magnificent body of water. It is so clear that it looks like pure alcohol." (Courtesy of RHM.)

At the east end of Silver Springs Creek, near where it joined Spring Creek, Harvey improved the waterfall. The stonework and wooden bridge around the lower falls created a popular place for visiting couples. (Courtesy of RHM.)

None of the Monte Ne springs were farther than a few feet from the banks of the creek. Harvey added wooden walkways around the banks for those who chose to walk rather than boat. On the bank of Elixir Spring, almost directly below the spot where the Missouri Row hotel would later be constructed, a limestone retaining wall was built. (Courtesy of RHM.)

Around each of the springs, Harvey built small boardwalks, which were popular places for picnics and family gatherings. The cold spring water was an added refreshment. Harvey noted that the water "is delicious to drink and slakes the thirst perfectly." (Top courtesy of RHM; bottom courtesy of SMOH/Betty Swearingen.)

Tourists to Monte Ne could walk around the lake and lagoon on the boardwalks and picnic by the springs. Harvey also developed lakeside and creekside parks, lush green areas for outdoor activities. (Courtesy of RHM.)

Adding to the idyllic nature of the Monte Ne valley was an abundance of wildlife. Visitors enjoyed birdwatching and feeding the waterfowl, while sportsmen relished frequent fox hunts. (Top courtesy of RHM; bottom courtesy of SMOH/Howard Clark.)

In about 1905, Josephine (left) and Hazel Hummel were photographed on the carriage road to Monte Ne. Harvey held a mass meeting of Rogers citizens in November 1900 to discuss financing improvements in the carriage road. But many Rogers business owners felt an easy-to-reach Monte Ne might take away their customers, and they failed to support road upgrades. (Courtesy of RHM.)

Small, temporary, wooden bridges were constructed to cross the lagoon until permanent structures could be built. These women, about 1901, were enjoying their visit by taking in the fresh air around the waters. (Courtesy of SMOH/Karen Armstrong.)

Three stone-and-concrete bridges were built across the lagoon. A bridge with eight battlement piers (top) took Fred Taylor and John Silcott about four months to complete in 1901. It crossed the lagoon at Fourth Street, at the north end of the lake and just south of where Oklahoma Row was eventually constructed. During Monte Ne's grand opening on May 4, 1901, the *Rogers Democrat* described the bridge as "substantial and graceful" and said it "will represent the main entrance to the grounds from the north." The simpler stone bridge (bottom) and its twin were located just south of where the first hotel, Hotel Monte Ne, was built and served as the main walkways for hotel guests to reach some of the lakeside parks. (Courtesy of RHM.)

Even in its heyday, Monte Ne's downtown only consisted of a handful of businesses. Here a group of picnickers gathers at a shady spot between the lagoon and a downtown shop, about 1901. (Courtesy of RHM.)

Harvey began building his resort in earnest in 1901, but it was always the simplicity of the water of Silver Springs Creek and the scenery that enticed most visitors. "The foliage at Monte Ne is magnificent," Harvey wrote in November 1900. "There is an abundance of shade for the sunniest days, with the pleasant rustle of the breeze-fanned leaves crooning an accompaniment." (Courtesy of SMOH/Ada Lee Shook.)

Three

HOTELS, TRAINS, AND BOATS

As news of the resort began to spread through Northwest Arkansas, more and more local folks made the journey down to the valley. Here the Powell family and friends from Rogers gather at their horse-drawn buggy. From left to right, the visitors were (standing) Alice Powell, Tallah Powell, Dorothy Powell, Ethel Powell, and Charlie Milligan; (in vehicle) Leon Powell, Mabel Martin, Edwin Powell, and Harry Powell. (Courtesy of SMOH/Betty Swearingen.)

To house visitors before permanent buildings were erected, E. H. Raymond of Oklahoma created a tent hotel, locals opened their cottages to renters, and James Balcom opened the Geneva Hotel on his property (top), later renamed the Sanders House. The first permanent resort facility was Hotel Monte Ne (bottom), a three-story, frame building with two 300-foot wings. The construction contract was given in December 1900 to the Rogers Lumber Company, and it was completed in April 1901. Each guest room in the hotel had an outside entrance. Meals, or "table board," were served, if desired, in the dining room at the east end of the hotel (left). (Top courtesy of SMOH; bottom courtesy of RHM.)

Hotel Monte Ne fronted the lagoon with a series of broad wooden stairs built down to the waterside (top). Rates, according to Harvey, were "very reasonable." The grand opening of the Monte Ne resort took place on May 4, 1901, with a ball in the dining room and hundreds of Japanese lanterns lighting the porches. The grounds surrounding the hotel were improved in the spring of 1905 with flower beds and roses, creating what the *Rogers Democrat* called "a perfect picture of beauty." (Top courtesy of SMOH; bottom courtesy of SMOH/Dock Hinson.)

Socializing on the hotel's wide porches (also called promenades) was one of the highlights of a visit to the resort. As was the case at popular resorts in other sections of the country, part of the reason for spending time at a resort was to see and to be seen. "The accommodations at Monte Ne are excellent," Harvey wrote. "Hotel Monte Ne is new and correspondingly modern. Its table is appetizing; its rooms are ample, well-appointed, and perfectly ventilated." (Courtesy of RHM.)

Harvey advertised Monte Ne as a relaxing, restful getaway: "Monte Ne is not a . . . crowded resort, where thoughtless people keep others awake at nighttime. It is a place where fashionable dressing is not expected—an elegant, quiet, restful place." (Courtesy of SMOH.)

E. H. Raymond gave up his tent hotel and became the manager of Hotel Monte Ne. He was assisted by Mrs. Lou Burgess from Chicago and Mr. and Mrs. J. E. Sanders, who served as cook and housekeeper. Although out-of-town visitors primarily stayed at the hotel, locals came to Monte Ne, too, including Vivian Kruse (center) and her friends from Rogers, shown about 1910. (Courtesy of RHM.)

Even in later years (here in the 1940s), local folks found that Monte Ne was an excellent place for a family reunion, picnic, or just a relaxing Sunday. This family is standing to the east of Hotel Monte Ne among several cairns, stone piles marking the drop down to the lagoon. (Courtesy of RHM.)

In March 1901, Harvey commissioned a theme song for his resort. Edward Wolfe of Rogers wrote "Beautiful Monte Ne," which Harvey copyrighted in 1906. Its chorus is: "Beautiful Monte Ne, God's gift to man they say / Health resort of all the world is beautiful Monte Ne / Rosy cheeks and purer blood they gain there day by day / In mountain air and water rare at beautiful Monte Ne." (Courtesy of RHM.)

In August 1901, Harvey wrote to his wife, Anna, "Everything here including my solvency depends upon the building of the railroad." His brother Thomas and many local folks helped with the financing; Harvey looked to both nearby towns, Rogers and Lowell, for help as well. Lowell agreed, and Harvey incorporated the Monte Ne Railway Company in May 1902 with a capital stock of $250,000. "Gangs of hill men," according to W. T. McWhorter, laid 14,000 oak railroad ties (seen here being delivered to Monte Ne) and 56-pound rail through Cross Hollows, south of Rogers, to the Lowell transfer station (bottom) to create the five-mile private railroad spur. Harvey bought an engine, tender, and passenger coach from the St. Louis and San Francisco (Frisco) Railroad, probably Frisco 4-4-0 No. 41, which the Frisco sold in May 1902. (Top courtesy of SMOH; bottom courtesy of RHM.)

At the south end of Big Spring Lake, Harvey built what the *Rogers Democrat* called an "old-fashioned log cabin" depot flanked by open-air waiting rooms (top). Possibly influenced by seeing gondolas at the 1893 Columbian Exposition in Chicago, Harvey then imported a 50-foot gondola (bottom) from Venice, Italy, in July 1901. Dante Moretti, its owner, came to set up the canal boat and teach gondolier Vern Ingersoll how to operate it. Although Ingersoll never sang while oaring, others may have. Gondola rides cost about 10¢ per person for an evening ride. Ever the marketer, Harvey widely promoted Monte Ne as "the only place in America where a gondola meets the train." An image of a gondola even graced the top of Monte Ne railroad passes. (Top courtesy of SMOH/Bob Besom; bottom courtesy of RHM.)

Harvey wrote about his transportation system: "Think of stepping from a train into a gondola. Who ever heard of such a thing in this lakeless island region of the southwest! It's enough to make one rub one's eyes and wonder if the glistening water and picturesque craft are real. Think of all the resorts you've ever seen or heard of. Picture the hot, dusty ride from the railway station to the hotel. (That will not be difficult.) Then compare the way they do at Monte Ne—a few steps across the platform, a comfortable seat in a gondola or launch and a dustless, joltless ride over a half-mile stretch of cool, transparent water, alighting close to the veranda of a modern, well-equipped hotel. Does it sound like a fairy tale?" (Top courtesy of SMOH/Mrs. Kenneth Tillotson; bottom courtesy of RHM.)

The gondola, also called a swanboat for its distinctive prow and stern, was perhaps the most popular boat at Monte Ne. It could hold up to 25 people. The gondoliers learned early how to steer the gondola and to pass under Monte Ne's three stone bridges (top) without losing the 10-foot oar. Occasionally the gondola was fitted with a canvas tarp to ward off the summer sun (bottom). Dante Moretti and Harry Pries from St. Louis brought another boat to Monte Ne in 1905, a gasoline launch dubbed *The Major Blackburn* (pictured in front of the Hotel Monte Ne on page 26). It was a four-horsepower, gas-powered motorboat that could travel up to 12 miles per hour. Moretti and Pries were involved with the "water concessions" at the 1904 St. Louis World's Fair. (Top courtesy of SMOH; bottom courtesy of RHM.)

The grand opening of the railroad was June 19, 1902. Harvey hoped to draw a crowd by inviting his friend and politician William Jennings Bryan, seen here (center) with Harvey (left) and Perry Clark from Rogers (right). A heavy rain that morning discouraged many visitors so attendance was less than Harvey had anticipated. A morning presentation by local speakers formally celebrated the rail line's completion. The weather cleared up in the afternoon, and Bryan presented an address; attendance was even smaller than in the morning as "the crowd was largely of young folks who were there for fun." Another feature was a drill by 17 girls from Lowell. They represented the 1896 "Sixteen to One" silver-to-gold campaign slogan of Bryan and Harvey, with 16 girls dressed in white and a single girl wearing a gold dress. An evening dance held at the hotel with the Bentonville, Arkansas, cornet band was obviously a success since, according to newspaperman Erwin Funk, "the Rogers crowd did not get home until after two o'clock in the morning." (Courtesy of RHM.)

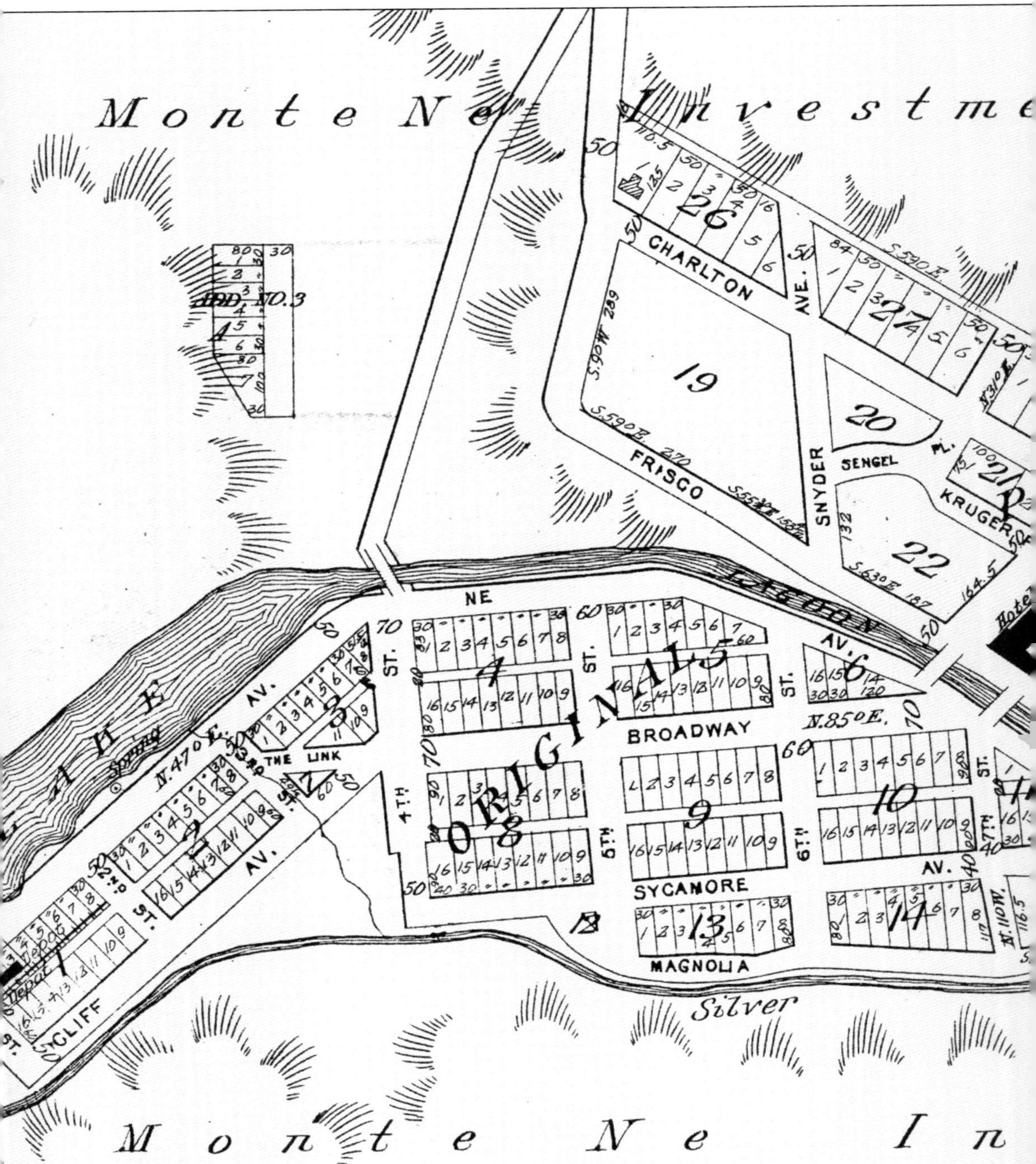

In December 1900, Harvey formed the Monte Ne Investment Company, to which all of the land he bought was deeded. Individuals invested $52,000 while Harvey contributed $48,000. Harvey's money came primarily from his book sales in the 1890s, especially *Coin's Financial School*, which sold several million copies. Monte Ne was platted four times, this one platted in April 1903 and published in the 1903 Benton County atlas. North-south streets were given number names, east-

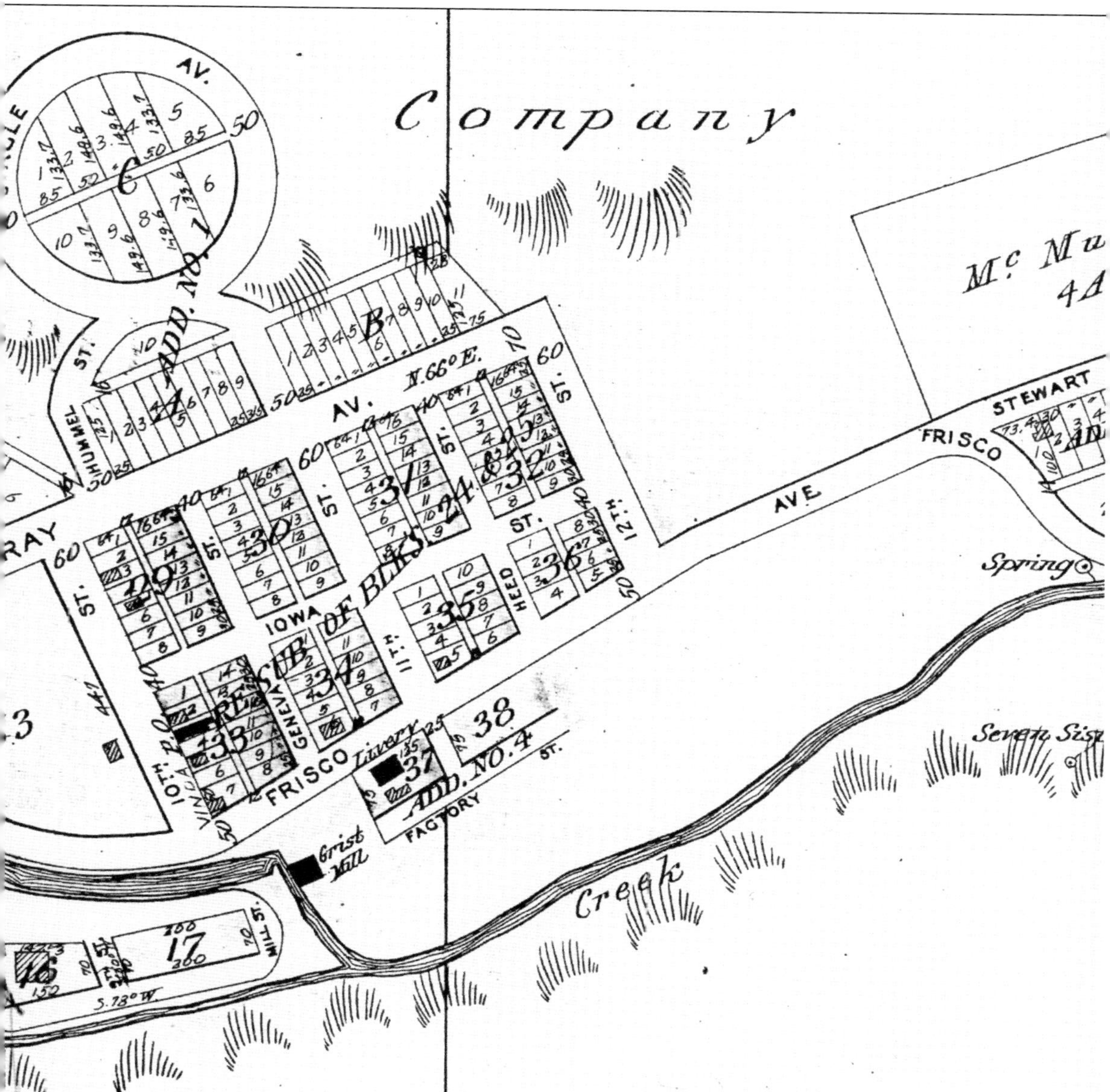

west streets a variety of names. The lake, lagoon, and many of the springs are shown on the map. The small black shapes represent buildings, including (from left to right) the train depot, Hotel Monte Ne, the post office, the gristmill, and a livery. In April 1901, Harvey was seeking industries to move onto Monte Ne's Factory Street by the livery, but few responded. (Courtesy of RHM.)

Peter Hummel came to Monte Ne in 1901 from Iowa and bought a farm near Monte Ne. In March 1901, he bought three lots at Monte Ne and built this livery barn, where owners kept their horses and where horses and carriages were rented out. (Courtesy of SMOH.)

In April 1901, the post office erroneously changed the town's name to Vinda, a misreading of Vinola, a nearby wine ranch. However, the name was soon formally changed to Monte Ne, and mail was delivered to this store and post office run by Peter Hummel's son Charles. (Courtesy of SMOH.)

For the July 4 celebration in 1902, a cornet band from Missouri played and Arkansas governor Jeff Davis gave an address before a crowd of 4,000. Many notables from Monte Ne gathered for this photograph on the steps of Hotel Monte Ne. Those present were, from left to right, (first row) Alex Sigmon, Governor Davis, P. B. Hummel, and Lewis Archer (standing); (second row) Arlie Starck, Carl A. Starck, Willie Ramsey, James Eden, Ike Hummel, and unidentified; (third row) Bob Ramsey, J. W. Sigmon, Jonathan Eden, Jerome Cowan, unidentified, George Graham, unidentified, and Pete M. Grisley (postmaster); (fourth row) unidentified, Norman Ingersoll, Silas Ingram, and Frank Ingram; (fifth row) ? Sanders, C. P. Hummel, Charles Kempton, Tom Harvey (Harvey's son), Tony LeBlanc, Miss J. E. Hix, unidentified, William "Coin" Harvey, unidentified, Halliday Harvey (Harvey's son), and ? Sanders. (Courtesy of the Butler Center for Arkansas Studies, Central Arkansas Library System, Little Rock, Arkansas.)

In late 1900, Harvey moved into the old Bailey home, a log house that, according to newspaperman Erwin Funk, was "built soon after the [Civil] War" and in need of repair. Son Tom arrived in November and helped Harvey prepare the house for the rest of the family still living in Chicago. In May 1901, Hal left law school and arrived at Monte Ne with his mother, Anna, and sister Annette. (Sister Hope married in 1901 and was living in New York.) Seven months later, sparks from an open fireplace burned down the house along with all the family's possessions, their dog, and a "large library" of Harvey's books, totaling some $2,500. Harvey carried no insurance on the home, and afterward Anna and Annette returned to Chicago. With the exception of a few, quick visits primarily to see her sons, Anna did not return to Monte Ne. After 25 years of marriage, Anna and Coin became permanently estranged. When son Hal was killed in a railroad accident in Oklahoma in October 1903, Harvey built a mausoleum near the lagoon as his resting place. (Courtesy of RHM.)

Four

The Club House Hotel and Cottage Company

In April 1904, Harvey organized the Monte Ne Club House Hotel and Cottage Company with capital stock of $250,000. He brought in A. O. Clarke from St. Louis to serve as architect and superintendent of the company. Harvey's intent was to build five large hotels: a three-story main building called the Club House Hotel and four 300-to-450-foot-long "cottage rows," each to be named for states surrounding Arkansas. The main building, pictured here but never built, was to be "as palatial as a Roman imperial villa." It reportedly was to include one room with an 18-foot waterfall. (Courtesy of SMOH.)

Stockholders in the Club House Hotel and Cottage Company received stock certificates like this one. "Privileges and Conditions" mentioned on the back include transportation on the Monte Ne Railroad (Lowell to Monte Ne), along with 150 pounds of baggage and a 25 percent discount for the stockholder and his family at Monte Ne hotels. (Courtesy of RHM.)

Missouri Row on the Lagoon, Monte Ne, Ark.

Missouri Row was the first hotel constructed, beginning in August 1904. The Clarke-designed building was 46 feet wide and 305 feet long and built of 8,000 hewn logs with a cement floor and red-tile roof. Fourteen thousand cubic feet of concrete were used. The tiles alone were shipped from Chicago in five railroad cars. The center and two ends of the hotel rose to two stories, the remainder being a single story. As was the case with Hotel Monte Ne, Missouri Row featured long porches—575 feet of them. The hotel boasted 40 sixteen-foot-square rooms, each with a fireplace to ward off the chill on summer nights in the valley. The hotel claimed it could accommodate "200 extra people on cots when occasion requires it." (Courtesy of RHM.)

Harvey employed area carpenters and stonemasons to build Missouri Row. In April 1905, to save time and money, the work schedule was changed from 9 to 10 hours per day and some wages were cut. Many workers went on strike and, when their demands were not met, quit. The strike delayed construction, but by the end of May, a full workforce was in place. In July, carpet, washstands, and furniture, including iron-and-brass bedsteads, were installed in the rooms. The *Rogers Democrat* reported that "cannon balls and shells from Pea Ridge battlefield are sunk in the cement porch floor on either side of the main entrance." Missouri Row opened in September 1905. Guest rates upon opening were $1 a day or $6 a week. (Courtesy of RHM.)

Many of the first arrivals to Missouri Row were families of stockholders taking advantage of their discounted hotel rates, but later people began to arrive from across the country. While most out-of-town guests arrived via the Monte Ne Railway, local visitors, such as Dr. W. A. McHenry from Rogers (bottom), traveled by horse and buggy. (Courtesy of RHM.)

Along with gatherings on the porches, visitors enjoyed strolls and playing games such as croquet on the wide, 300-foot lawn west of Missouri Row. Today this lawn area is totally covered in trees and brush. (Courtesy of SMOH/Washington County Historical Society.)

In February 1907, with nearly 300 new stockholders, Harvey began construction of his next hotel, Oklahoma Row, also designed by A. O. Clarke. Set to the west of Missouri Row with a wide lawn between them, Oklahoma Row had a similar log, cement, stone, and tile construction. The dining room was on the north end (top, at right), a large hall was at the center entrance, and a three-story concrete tower sat at the south end. Each of the 40 rooms had fireplaces, as did the dining room and center hall. Every room featured electric lights, sewerage, and running spring water. Work went slowly, however, and Harvey was desperate for additional cash. He wrote to his wife in June 1908, "I am trying to save the ship from sinking." (Top courtesy of SMOH/Eva Graves; bottom courtesy of SMOH.)

By July 1908, Harvey was in dire financial straights. Writing to son Tom, he said, "I have not yet paid all my taxes and am threatened with forfeiture of all my charters. I have defaulted on interest. . . . The Club Company has no money and is overdrawn. The season is a failure—we now have only five guests in the house and the season promises to close at a loss." By March 1909, however, Harvey had raised enough money to finish Oklahoma Row, but it opened without a gala event. Like Missouri Row, Oklahoma Row had 600 feet of porches where guests frequently lounged, socialized, and entertained. Oklahoma and Missouri Rows were in their day the two largest log buildings in the world. (Courtesy of RHM.)

The various building projects at Monte Ne had made Harvey a strong advocate of Portland cement, which was at that time still in limited use in the United States. For Oklahoma Row's construction, which took between 35,000 and 40,000 cubic feet of stone and cement, metal reinforced concrete was used to construct the foundation, basement, fireplaces, and a three-story tower on the south end of the hotel. The tower, one of the earliest multistory concrete buildings in the country, was accessed by a stairway rising from the log section of the building. From the west side of the building, visitors could look out over the lagoon, and those in the tower could see all the way to the railway depot. (Courtesy of RHM.)

Rooms in Oklahoma Row, as in Missouri Row, each featured fireplaces and many appointments. In 1910, the daily rates were $2.50 per day or $10 and up weekly, with meals costing 50¢. Harvey promoted the sophistication of Monte Ne by advertising in his resort publications the many other fine hotels nationally managed by stockholders of the Club House Hotel and Cottage Company. (Courtesy of SMOH.)

Five

RESORT AMENITIES

A 1902 Monte Ne advertisement said, "And what is there to do at Monte Ne? Well, to start with, there are charming walks and drives and rides. A good livery service is maintained, with comfortable carriages. . . . Then there are bowling alleys and billiard and pool rooms, and kindred amusements. There is a fine swimming pool . . . [and] an auditorium with a seating capacity of 500. . . . There is a large dancing pavilion where regular parties are given. White River, less than a mile away, affords the best of fishing." (Courtesy of SMOH.)

In August 1901, Harvey's son Hal and brother-in-law Ernest Halliday opened a large bathhouse on Silver Springs Creek across the lagoon from Hotel Monte Ne. The indoor pool, or "plunge bath," was the first in Arkansas. Measuring 25 by 50 feet and 7 feet deep, it included springboards and slides. Water from the spring flowed into the swimming pool, half of which was sectioned off and featured heated water piped in from a wood-fired boiler. The bathhouse had individual bathing and dressing rooms. A two-lane bowling alley was at the other end of the building. The pool cost 25¢, with 25¢ additional for rental of a bathing suit and towel. Brochures noted that "the state law requires bathing suits for ladies to be regulation cuts and modest." (Top courtesy of SMOH; bottom courtesy of RHM.)

The local papers frequently noted that the swimming pool was the most popular place in Monte Ne. In July 1910, the *Rogers Democrat* reported that there was "a flourishing business every Sunday." The Hummel family ran the pool in later years, and even when the resort failed to draw many tourists, the bathhouse often brought in over 200 swimmers a day. By the mid-1920s, however, outdoor bathing was again popular and the Willola outdoor swimming pool, which opened in 1923 just at the foot of the Monte Ne valley, drew away many swimmers from Monte Ne. (Courtesy of SMOH/Marion S. Warner.)

Boating and picnicking along the lagoon continued to be popular pastimes at Monte Ne. The gondola (top) was still the most popular boat ride, but johnboats and the gasoline launch also plied the lagoon and lake. Boardwalks around the lagoon and by the springs (bottom) became favorite spots for group photographs. (Top courtesy of SMOH/Karen Armstrong; bottom courtesy of RHM.)

Harvey frequently stocked the lake and lagoon to assure guests' success when fishing. The state fish commissioner stocked the waters with rainbow trout, while the Neosho, Missouri, fish commissioner brought 10,000 fish for the lake in May 1905. (Courtesy of RHM.)

Another popular sport at Monte Ne was fox hunting. The hunts drew participants from as far as Missouri and Oklahoma and continued into the mid-1920s. One meeting of the Fox Hunters Association in 1908 drew 100 people. (Courtesy of SMOH.)

Harvey also worked to foster a festive spirit at the resort by sponsoring concerts and fiddling contests. Music frequently filled the air but not always at the auditorium. For example, visitors could enjoy a Fayetteville band playing on the boardwalk by Big Spring. (Courtesy of RHM.)

Although Northwest Arkansas was almost exclusively white in the early 20th century, African American musicians could arrive by train during the day, entertain on the steps of Hotel Monte Ne, and take the train out of town by day's end. (Courtesy of SMOH.)

The auditorium hosted concerts and dances, as did the Monte Ne dance pavilion built by C.P. Hummel. Weekly dances were popular through the mid-1920s. Occasionally the dances got out of control, such as happened in November 1905 when the *Rogers Democrat* reported: "The conduct and actions of a number of people, both men and women—especially women—at a dance in Monte Ne last Saturday night deserves severe condemnation. Drunkenness is bad for men to indulge in, and for women it is doubly disgusting." Harvey used the *Monte Ne Herald*, the newspaper he started in April 1904, which was edited by Tom Harvey and Tony LeBlanc, to publicize events such as concerts. The newspaper office was on the second floor of the railway depot. The last issue of the newspaper was published in May 1905, probably due as much to financial problems as to unpleasantries following Harvey's publication of some personal attacks. (Courtesy of RHM/Thelma Graham.)

A popular sport at the turn of the 20th century, tennis also found its way to Monte Ne. The wide, flat lawn between Missouri and Oklahoma Rows (top) provided an excellent grass court for "lawn tennis" as well as for croquet. These young women (bottom) in about 1901 are wearing the latest in tennis fashion. (Top courtesy of RHM; bottom courtesy of SMOH/Karen Armstrong.)

A golf course east of downtown Monte Ne (top), created sometime before 1909, is believed to be the first golf course in Northwest Arkansas. Golf was a fairly new form of recreation at the turn of the 20th century (the first U.S. golf courses opened in the 1880s), so the availability of the sport at Monte Ne is significant. From the photograph, it is obvious that the hills of Monte Ne made for a challenging course. A golf tournament accompanied the formal dedication of Oklahoma Row in August 1909. A new golf course was built in 1928. (Courtesy of RHM.)

East of the hotels was Monte Ne's small downtown with a few businesses and stores. C. P. Hummel and his brother, Clinton, erected the two-story frame building with porch in May 1901 to serve as a general mercantile store and post office. In 1907, C. P. ordered 100,000 picture postcards of Monte Ne to sell. He ran the store until his death in 1921, when it was taken over by Josephine and Berry Graham, Hummel's daughter and son-in-law. Both C. P. Hummel and his wife, Alice, served a number of years as postmaster, as did their daughter, Josephine. Kenneth Doescher, the last Monte Ne postmaster, remembered, "Not everything in Monte Ne revolved around the tourists. . . . School plays were held above Hummel's store, a place that was also used for a Masonic Lodge and community affairs." (Courtesy of SMOH/Howard Clark.)

The Monte Ne Mercantile Company opened in 1905. Harvey began issuing his own money, or scrip, which was accepted and used as cash in and around Monte Ne. Scrip was a way of financing his mercantile without the necessity of operating capital. Harvey would purchase items (for example, a truckload of vegetables from local farmers). Instead of paying with federal currency, he paid in scrip, which he promised to redeem within 30 days after the purchased item (the vegetables) sold. If the item did not sell, then the scrip had no value. (Courtesy of RHM.)

In October 1905, Harvey organized the Bank of Monte Ne. Architect A. O. Clarke designed the concrete, two-story building (50 by 70 feet), which included the bank and a storeroom on the main floor and a lodge room and several offices on the second. The building was in downtown Monte Ne, just across the street from and west of the post office. The bank opened in January 1906, and in June, the Interstate Bankers' Summer Club, a group of bankers from the Southwest, met at Monte Ne. By 1907, however, Harvey was running advertisements in the local papers appealing to the "friends of Monte Ne" for their patronage. Among the organizations that used the upstairs was a local Odd Fellows lodge. (Courtesy of RHM.)

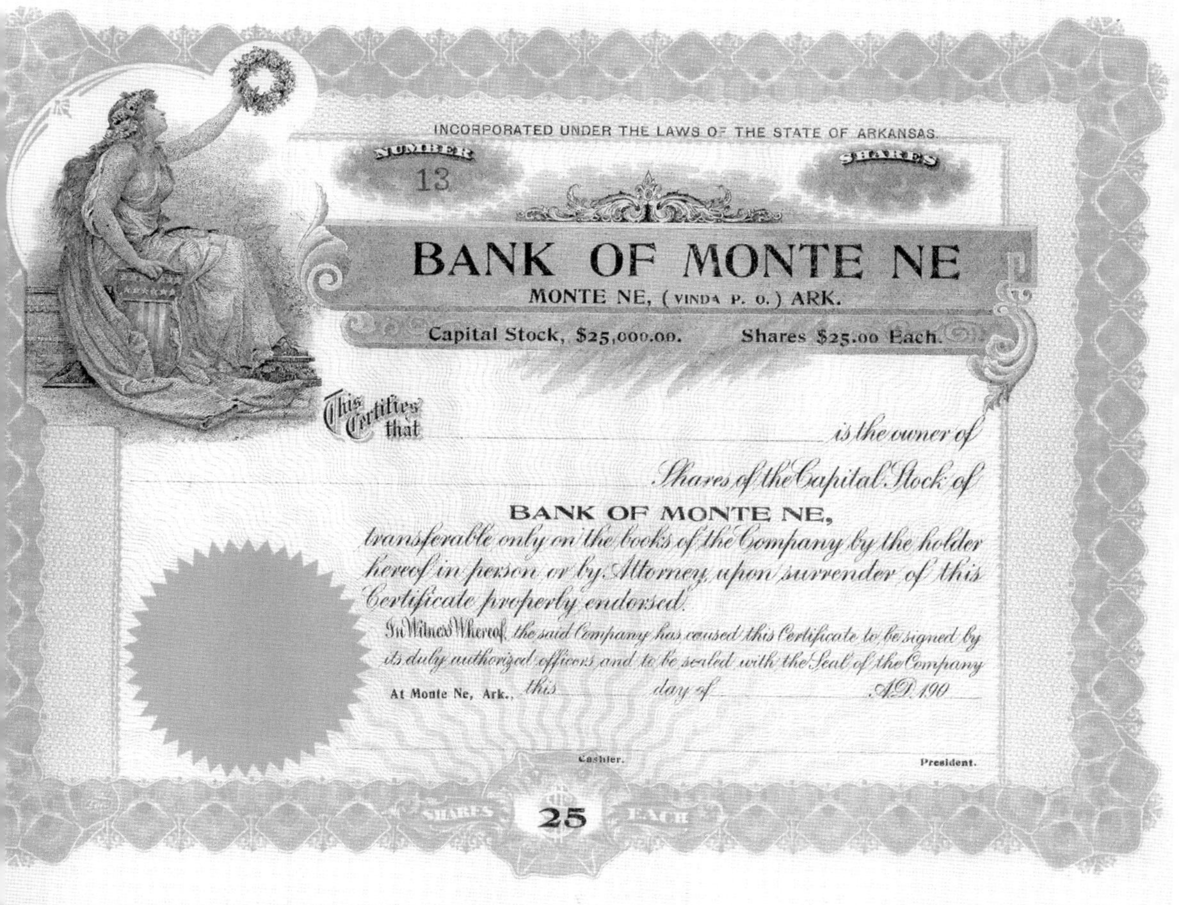

INCORPORATED UNDER THE LAWS OF THE STATE OF ARKANSAS.

NUMBER 13 SHARES

BANK OF MONTE NE

MONTE NE, (VINDA P. O.) ARK.

Capital Stock, $25,000.00. Shares $25.00 Each.

This Certifies that ______ is the owner of ______ Shares of the Capital Stock of

BANK OF MONTE NE,

transferable only on the books of the Company by the holder hereof in person or by Attorney upon surrender of this Certificate properly endorsed.

In Witness Whereof, the said Company has caused this Certificate to be signed by its duly authorized officers and to be sealed with the Seal of the Company

At Monte Ne, Ark., this ______ day of ______ A.D. 190__

Cashier. President.

SHARES 25 EACH

Harvey created the Bank of Monte Ne, capitalized at $25,000, by issuing stock. For $15 per share, stockholders could buy into the bank. This blank stock certificate was probably from the bank's earliest years, 1906 to 1909. (Courtesy of SMOH.)

This bird's-eye view of Monte Ne from the east shows the downtown, including the bank (the large windowed building near center) in 1907 or 1908. To the very left, partially hidden by trees, is the Silver Springs grist and flour mill. Pictured in the distance just above the bank is Oklahoma Row, whose tower is peeking out from behind the trees. Downtown Monte Ne never got much bigger than this. (Courtesy of SMOH/Bob Besom.)

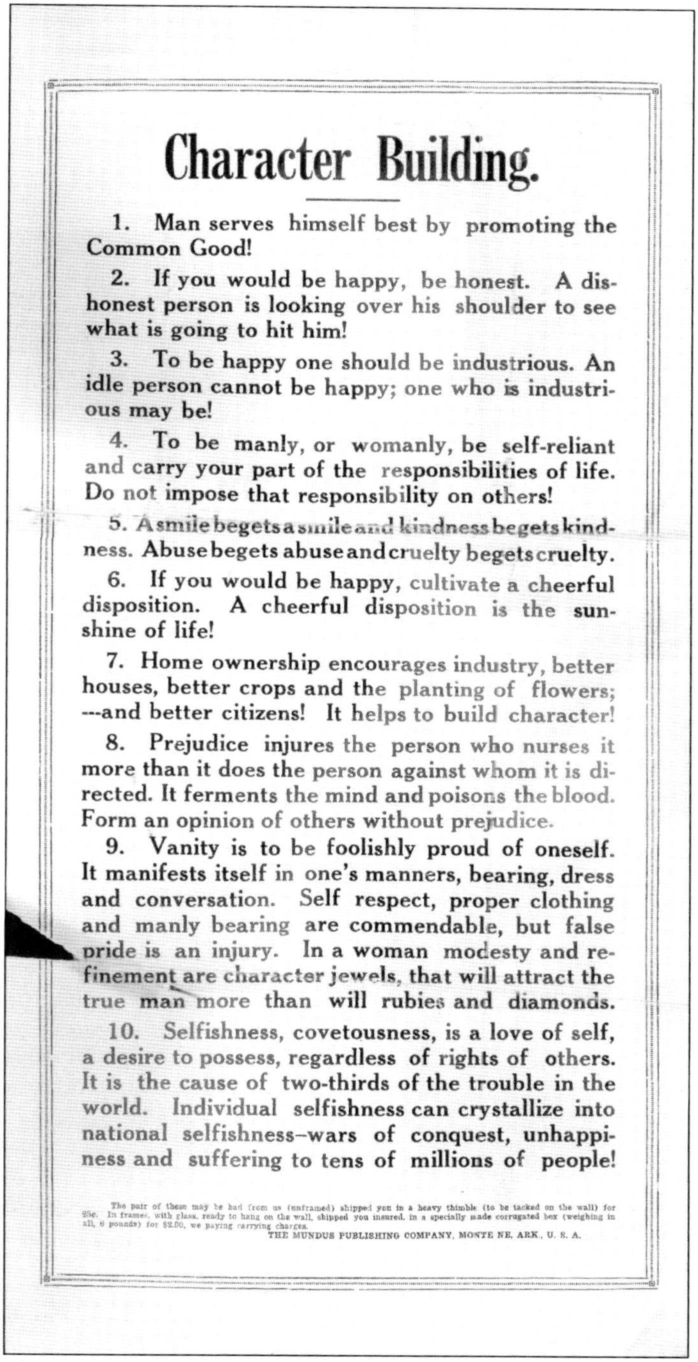

Character Building.

1. Man serves himself best by promoting the Common Good!

2. If you would be happy, be honest. A dishonest person is looking over his shoulder to see what is going to hit him!

3. To be happy one should be industrious. An idle person cannot be happy; one who is industrious may be!

4. To be manly, or womanly, be self-reliant and carry your part of the responsibilities of life. Do not impose that responsibility on others!

5. A smile begets a smile and kindness begets kindness. Abuse begets abuse and cruelty begets cruelty.

6. If you would be happy, cultivate a cheerful disposition. A cheerful disposition is the sunshine of life!

7. Home ownership encourages industry, better houses, better crops and the planting of flowers; ---and better citizens! It helps to build character!

8. Prejudice injures the person who nurses it more than it does the person against whom it is directed. It ferments the mind and poisons the blood. Form an opinion of others without prejudice.

9. Vanity is to be foolishly proud of oneself. It manifests itself in one's manners, bearing, dress and conversation. Self respect, proper clothing and manly bearing are commendable, but false pride is an injury. In a woman modesty and refinement are character jewels, that will attract the true man more than will rubies and diamonds.

10. Selfishness, covetousness, is a love of self, a desire to possess, regardless of rights of others. It is the cause of two-thirds of the trouble in the world. Individual selfishness can crystallize into national selfishness–wars of conquest, unhappiness and suffering to tens of millions of people!

The pair of these may be had from us (unframed) shipped you in a heavy thimble (to be tacked on the wall) for 25c. In frames, with glass, ready to hang on the wall, shipped you insured, in a specially made corrugated box (weighing in all, 6 pounds) for $2.00, we paying carrying charges.

THE MUNDUS PUBLISHING COMPANY, MONTE NE, ARK., U. S. A.

Having taught school when he was 16 years old, Harvey continued to be interested in education. In 1904, he wrote a book on "Character Teaching" to be used in the public schools. It focused on three principles: industriousness, self-reliance, and the common good. In July 1916, Harvey convened a Character Building Conference at Monte Ne. Educators from eight states attended, as well as Arkansas governor-elect Hillman Brough. (Courtesy of RHM.)

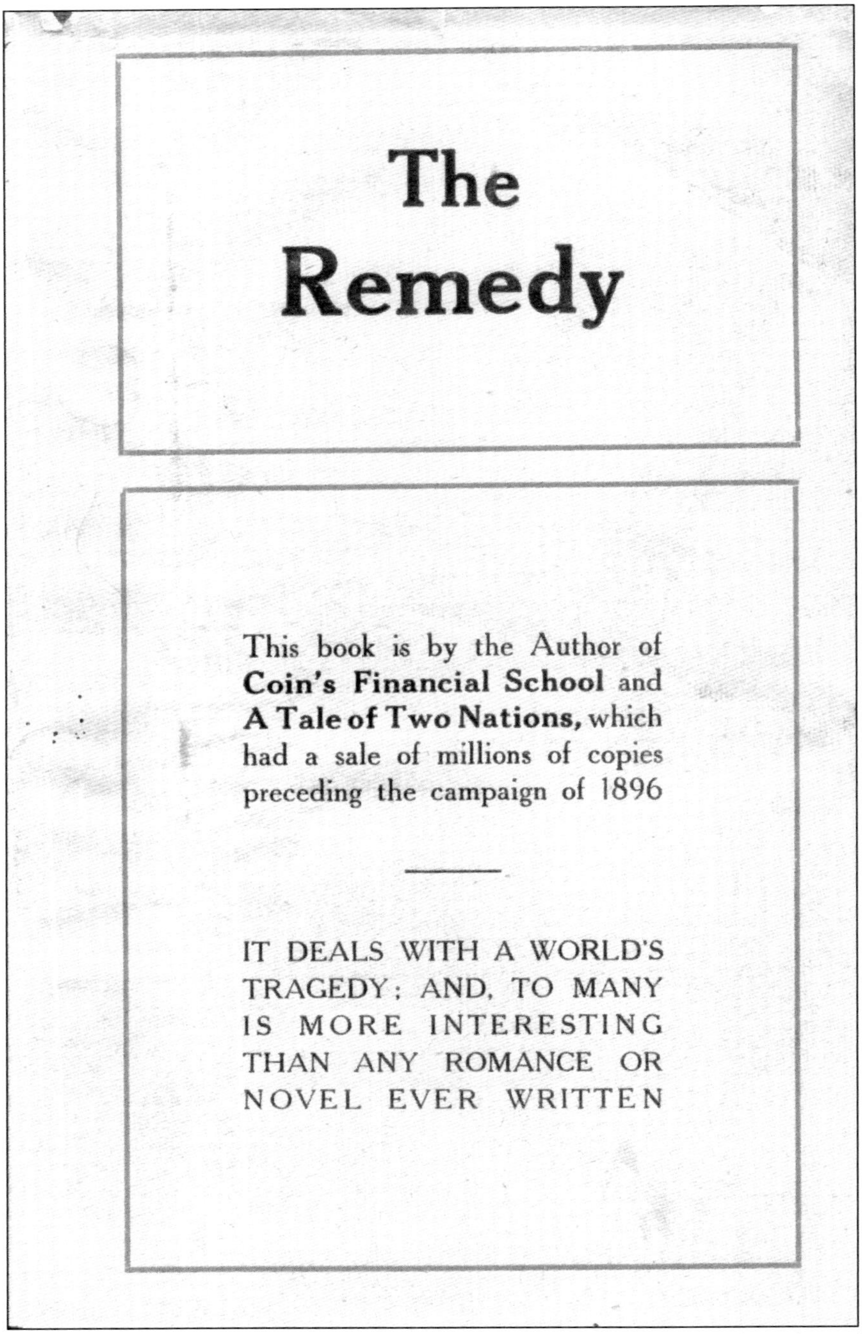

The Remedy

This book is by the Author of **Coin's Financial School** and **A Tale of Two Nations,** which had a sale of millions of copies preceding the campaign of 1896

IT DEALS WITH A WORLD'S TRAGEDY; AND, TO MANY IS MORE INTERESTING THAN ANY ROMANCE OR NOVEL EVER WRITTEN

In 1915, Harvey published *The Remedy*, based on his 1904 work, which advocated teaching character building in schools. He sent copies to the German kaiser, the czar of Russia, the president and premier of France, King George V, and the rest of the European rulers, along with one to Pres. Woodrow Wilson. Harvey believed that teaching character building would address world ills. "By a test of the increasing number in crimes, suicides, insanity, tenantry, and divorces, ours is now a declining civilization," Harvey wrote. (Courtesy of RHM.)

In the late 19th century, Silver Springs had a schoolhouse (top) where local children were educated. That schoolhouse continued to serve the community as the Monte Ne resort was being built. Continued growth of Monte Ne, however, necessitated a new, four-room schoolhouse (bottom), built for about $2,000. Teachers were advertised for in the *St. Louis Mirror*: "We are desirous of securing the services of about three good, competent men to teach the higher branches." Miss Etta Williams was the primary teacher from 1901 to at least 1904. (Courtesy of RHM.)

Harvey worked hard to attract tourists as well as home builders and businesses to Monte Ne, and he had many supporters through the years, especially the Hummel, Wayne, and Graham families. Pictured in 1931 are, from left to right, Harvey's grandson Richard Halliday, Harvey, Earl Wayne, unidentified, Minnie Graham, and Dixie Graham. However, many agreed with *Rogers Democrat* editor Erwin Funk that Harvey was "a difficult man to please." A popular story was that Harvey had a lights-out rule at 10:00 p.m. and that one weekend, when the hotel was full and the visitors were up late, Harvey turned off the main electrical switch. The next morning, the majority of the visitors packed their luggage and left. Some also criticized him for holding activities at Monte Ne on the Sabbath, others for banning children from the resort, and still others for asking anyone becoming ill at the resort to be taken somewhere else. Others even accused him of philandering. (Courtesy of RHM.)

Six

TRAILS AND AUTOMOBILES

Harvey worked tirelessly to upgrade the roads to Monte Ne. Most of the Rogers business community and many local landowners, however, believed that if they helped boost Monte Ne, it would draw business away from Rogers. Nonetheless, Harvey continued as a proponent of what was called the "good roads" movement. He had already seen the writing on the wall for the horse and buggy; in a 1911 speech he noted, "This is the day of Motor Power, and automobiles are becoming the established method of transportation over roads." (Courtesy of RHM.)

In 1910, Harvey conceived the idea of bringing a "vast network of modern auto routes" into Arkansas. In July 1913 at a Monte Ne convention, he announced the formation of the Ozark Trails Association (OTA) to promote better roads (but not to build them) and to mark them to assist travelers. That convention was at the time the largest gathering of automobiles ever seen in Northwest Arkansas. The meetings were held in the office of Oklahoma Row. Harvey has

been credited by some with being one of the earliest promoters of the nationwide "good roads" movement and the building of highways. Harvey's motivation, however, was not so altruistic. "My personal interest in the Ozark Trails," he wrote in 1913, "is that they all lead to Monte Ne." (Courtesy of SMOH/David Purdy.)

EXECUTIVE CHAMBER
State of Arkansas
LITTLE ROCK.

Certificate of Appointment

This is to Certify, *That, pursuant to the official call, I have appointed and commissioned, and do hereby appoint and commission*

C. P. Hammel

of Monte Ne *as a delegate to*

represent Ozark Trails Convention

at the Convention

which meets at Tulsa, Oklahoma

May 26 and 27 *A. D., 191*4

In Witness Whereof, *I have hereunto set my hand, in the Executive Chamber, City of Little Rock, on this the* 21st

day of May *A. D., 191*4

Geo W Hays

Governor

OTA delegates to the annual convention received an official "certificate of appointment" signed by the governor. This certificate certifies C. P. Hummel of Monte Ne as a delegate to the May 1914 convention in Tulsa, Oklahoma. (Courtesy of SMOH.)

Local residents worked on Monte Ne's roads. C. P. Hummel spent over $600 of his own money on the road to Rogers in 1915. But Harvey could not convince Rogers and Bentonville business owners to assist in the process. He went so far as to print brochures trying to shame them into subscribing and met with a Benton County judge, hoping to secure his motivational assistance, all for naught. At a stop in Rogers, OTA officer R. H. Whitlow said that "the people where [the OTA officers] have visited regard Col. Harvey as one of the biggest men in the Southwest and that it seems to be only here at home where there is little or no appreciation of the work he is accomplishing in the Ozark Trails ideas." (Top courtesy of SMOH/Bob Besom; bottom courtesy of Elizabeth Bigham Collection/Saunders Memorial Museum.)

In 1920, the OTA began to promote the building of road markers to indicate mileage to various towns and cities, and the markers took the form of small obelisks or, as they were called at the time, pyramids. Some towns through which the Ozark Trail passed have maintained their markers (top, Lake Arthur, New Mexico, in 2004). No local markers around the Monte Ne area seem to have been erected. However, one signpost from the Monte Ne resort area (bottom), still visible in 1961 before the flooding of Beaver Lake, takes the form of a truncated obelisk with a plate-iron arrow. This may have been an early version of the "pyramid" concept, or perhaps a local version of the markers. (Top courtesy of Richard Covey and Nan Lawler; bottom courtesy of James Maxwell Skipper.)

In 1919, the OTA published the official *Ozark Trails Route Book*, printed by the *Rogers Democrat*. In September 1920 alone, 10,000 copies of the book were mailed from Monte Ne. (Courtesy of RHM.)

At the October 1920 OTA convention, Harvey stepped down from the presidency, having served for seven years, although he continued to attend conventions and push for good roads (as did others, such as this local good-roads supporter in the 1920s). The 1921 convention was disrupted when some of the delegates walked out and left the organization, citing "we have had all the experience with Mr. Harvey we care to have." In the end, the main influence of the OTA was to encourage small towns to create good roads and promote tourism. By the 1920s, road improvements were being made nationwide, the price of cars had decreased, and the number of automobiles had increased. Americans began to replace long vacations at a single resort with driving to multiple sites and "auto camping" or staying overnight at motels. Monte Ne suffered the same fate as other resorts, facing a decreasing number of out-of-state and overnight guests. Northwest Arkansas residents, however, continued to visit Monte Ne as they always had, for recreation, social time, and cool temperatures. (Courtesy of SMOH/Robert G. Winn.)

Seven

Doom, Gloom, and the Pyramid

By 1920, Coin Harvey had suffered many setbacks and failures. His last child, Tom, left Monte Ne in 1908, and friend William Jennings Bryan failed to find a place for Harvey in the Woodrow Wilson administration. The Monte Ne Railway was sold, absorbed, put into receivership, and abandoned during World War I, and the rails were eventually torn up. Harvey had little local support for his good-roads projects. A bid in 1913 for the Third Congressional District seat of Arkansas failed, and the Bank of Monte Ne went out of business in 1914. (Courtesy of RHM.)

FOURTH EDITION

Common Sense

or

The CLOT on the BRAIN of the BODY POLITIC

By the AUTHOR of COIN'S FINANCIAL SCHOOL.

In View of Increasing Crime, Suicides and Insanity for God's Sake Read this Book

A Book in Magazine Form that Every One in the World Should Read

CIRCULATION, HERETOFORE, 2 MILLION 800 THOUSAND

1927

Mundus Publishing Company

Publishers

Monte Ne :: :: :: Arkansas

Single Copy . . . . . . 25 Cents

QUANTITY PRICES: 3 Copies for 40 Cents; 8 Copies for $1.00; 17 Copies for $2.00; 100 or More, 10 Cents Each

We pay postage or other carrying charges *Prices given are for them delivered to you*

If you have received this copy without ordering it, someone else has paid for it

Disheartened by misfortune, wary of the automobile's impact on the resort, concerned about his health, and disgusted with the state of the national economy and politics, Harvey's priorities changed in the 1920s. In February 1920, he published *Common Sense* (here in the 1927 fourth edition, which claimed a circulation of 2.8 million copies.). Its opening sentence introduced Harvey's new focus: "It is now evident to all that the world is face to face with the problem of the reconstruction of civilization." In the book, he fused several issues of concern to him: the public's failure to understand Harvey's ideas about money, the banking system, the "free silver" issue, and usury (charging interest on loans); and his "remedy": education, character building, and the fundamental principle of "free government" (equal opportunity, free speech, and independent citizens). Predicting that civilization was therefore doomed, Harvey announced in *Common Sense* his intention to leave a message for the future in the form of a "pyramid." (Courtesy of RHM.)

Harvey anticipated that at the catastrophic end of civilization, the mountains around his Monte Ne valley would crumble. To inform people in the future about what happened, Harvey planned to construct a 130-foot-high concrete obelisk, which he called the Pyramid. He believed that, after the cataclysm, people would find the Pyramid's capstone, and a plaque thereon would lead discoverers to dig down to its base. In two vaults in the shaft were to be placed Harvey's own books explaining 20th-century civilization, as well as a world globe, a Bible, encyclopedias, and newspapers, all printed on special paper and hermetically sealed in glass. In a large room at the Pyramid's base were to be placed "numerous small items now used by us in domestic and industrial life, from the size of a needle and safety pin up to a victrola [record player]." (Courtesy of RHM.)

With a 40-square-foot base, the Pyramid was to sit on a slight rise at the south end of Big Spring Lake. Harvey ran "expensive tunnels" beneath the area to check for possible sources of erosion. It was estimated that the construction would use 16,000 sacks of cement, 30,000 cubic feet of sand, 58,000 cubic feet of gravel, and tons of corrugated steel reinforcement. The Portland Cement Association donated the service of one of its experts, and he pronounced that the Pyramid would not deteriorate or suffer from erosion and would last a million years and longer. To prevent water in the valley from interfering with the foundation and to shore up the low knoll for the incredibly heavy Pyramid, Harvey constructed a 165-foot-long retaining wall of stone and cement, seen here during a drought in 2006. (Courtesy of James Maxwell Skipper.)

At the head of Big Spring Lake (top, looking southwest to that area) Harvey first built what was variously called the terrace, stadium, foyer, and entrance room to the Pyramid. In actuality, it was an amphitheater, a roughly semi-circular, terraced arena for seating, shown here (bottom) under construction in about 1928. The primary purpose of the amphitheater was the same as that of the retaining wall, to shore up the foundation of the Pyramid. (Top courtesy of James Maxwell Skipper; bottom courtesy of SMOH/Bob Besom.)

The land for the amphitheater was first dug in late 1923, and work continued off and on for the next five years as financing, building materials, and labor were available. Unlike other Monte Ne building projects that architect A. O. Clarke designed, the amphitheater apparently had no architect input and was not built according to blueprints or a single design. Those who worked with Harvey noted that he seemed to just "work it out in his mind from day to day." The result was a unique structure, irregular in formation, with seating capacity for anywhere from 500 to 1,000. The amphitheater averaged 20 feet high and 140 feet long. Harvey marked an "X" on a photograph of the amphitheater (bottom) to show where the Pyramid was to be erected. (Top courtesy of SMOH/Donna Charlesworth; bottom courtesy of RHM.)

While work was being undertaken on the amphitheater, Harvey built a high wooden fence around it on which he later wrote quotations from his books. He said he was forced to put up the fence "by the crowds that used the place as a picnic ground, left it covered with debris, and wrote their names and inscriptions all over the concrete work. [The fence] keeps the spring clean and pure." For 25¢, visitors could enter, view the progress being made, and listen to Harvey talk about his monetary theories and the state of the world. Visitors would receive a booklet about the Pyramid (one was published in 1925 and a second in 1928), and conveniently, a rack of Harvey's books were available for purchase. (Courtesy of SMOH/Washington County Historical Society.)

As was the case with other Harvey initiatives, he intended the cost of the amphitheater to be "shared" by taking subscriptions. In his 1925 booklet, "The Pyramid," Harvey wrote: "In designing and planning the Pyramid I had only contemplated the financing of it myself, but since its proposed construction was made public several have said to me that others would be glad to contribute to its cost." Harvey intended to place the names and addresses of those who contributed on parchment paper, which would be sealed in one of the Pyramid's vaults. Upon completion of the amphitheater, Harvey spent approximately $10,000 of his own funds and about $1,000 of voluntary contributions. (Top courtesy of SMOH/Herbert Holcomb; bottom courtesy of SMOH.)

In August 1928, Harvey dedicated the amphitheater before a crowd of about 500. The program featured music and an address by Harvey. The *Rogers Democrat* noted that Harvey "reverted to his old-time methods in his speech, that of a teacher and pupil, using three classes of students [from a local school] to illustrate . . . character building." The Pyramid project had been well published throughout the United States, and no doubt the idea of seeing a "pyramid," combined with the Egypt mania that held the country spellbound following the discovery of King Tut's tomb in 1922, also helped attract visitors to Monte Ne. Tens of thousands came to see Harvey's work over the years; more than 20,000 saw it within a single four-month period in 1928. (Top courtesy of RHM/Duane Hand; bottom courtesy of SMOH/Howard Clark.)

In the middle of Big Spring Lake, facing the amphitheater, Harvey placed a cement island, 15 by 30 feet, with a concrete "couch" and two "chairs" (top). This stage was intended as a place for an orchestra to play or a speaker to make a presentation. Harvey said that "the acoustics are marvelous; a speaker on this platform can be heard by all, speaking in a low voice." The square stone-and-concrete building (bottom) was originally a booth where visitors to the amphitheater would purchase tickets. (Top courtesy of RHM; bottom courtesy of RHM/Addie L. Colclasure and Juanita Tarpley.)

While work on the Pyramid continued, Harvey moved his office from Oklahoma Row to his cottage, just a stone's throw from the amphitheater. In 1924, he published *Paul's School of Statesmanship*, which advocated the abolition of usury, and continued to raise funds by letting out the amphitheater for events, such as conventions. In June 1930, Harvey installed a radio "for the entertainment of visitors." (Courtesy of SMOH/Arkansas State Publicity Department.)

In January 1929, Harvey incorporated the Pyramid Association, along with J. W. Kimmons of Lowell and H. L. Hardin of Kansas City. The association was to carry out Harvey's Pyramid plans in the event of his death. The estimated cost of the Pyramid itself was $75,000, but Harvey exhausted his funds on construction of the amphitheater and the Pyramid itself was never built. (Courtesy of RHM.)

Harvey's attention turned to the Pyramid project and away from the resort in the 1920s. Monte Ne's resort days were effectively over, and fewer and fewer visitors came from outside the area. But activities and events at Monte Ne very much continued, supported by local folks who still visited in large numbers. Harvey sold the former Hotel Monte Ne, which then became known as White Hotel (sometime prior to 1912), Randola Inn (1918), and Hotel Frances (1925), named for the daughter of owner R. H. Whitlow. Managers Joe Graham and Earl Wayne provided many amenities for guests, including orchestra concerts and lighted drives. The pool and dance pavilion were just across the lagoon. For a time beginning in 1930, the hotel was known as the Sleepy Valley Hotel. (Courtesy of RHM.)

Monte Ne's large log hotels continued to be active after they, along with the dance pavilion, about 10 acres, and Elixir Spring, were foreclosed and sold at public auction. From 1927 to 1932, Missouri and Oklahoma Rows (the latter more often then called the Club House Hotel) were home to the Ozark Industrial College and School of Theology, a nonsectarian school run by Dan W. Evans. The hotels housed pupils, seen here—Missouri Row for boys, Oklahoma Row for girls—and Oklahoma Row also provided classroom and dining space. Evans and his family lived in the tower. The dance pavilion was enclosed and served as the school chapel. In May 1932, a mortgage foreclosure against the school was brought; school officials were evicted, and the property was sold. (Courtesy of RHM/Lorene Huckstep.)

Picnics, swimming, lawn parties, dances, fox hunts, fiddling contests, banquets—area residents found Monte Ne in the 1920s the place to be, primarily in the spring and summer months but occasionally during the winter, too. A garage was opened in 1920 to accommodate the increasing number of driving visitors. A dance in July 1921 attracted several hundred. Camp Joyzelle, a girls' camp, opened in summer 1923 on land southeast of Big Spring Lake. Both in 1924 and 1925, the *Rogers Democrat* reported that the hotels had many guests and that the summer rental cottages were full. (Courtesy of RHM.)

Eight

Harvey's Waning Years

Coin Harvey was 69 years old when he announced his plans for the Pyramid. From about that time on, Harvey suffered a number of serious illnesses and injuries, yet he continued to work and take numerous business trips. Among other problems, he had blood poisoning in his foot in 1926, which resulted in several days' coma, surgery, and a three-month recuperation, and double pneumonia in 1930. In his later years (here at age 77), his eyes also failed him. He dealt with that by hiring young people to read the newspaper and letters to him. (Courtesy of AP/Wide World Photos.)

Coin and Anna were married in 1876, but they had been estranged since the 1901 house fire. In 1929, Anna agreed to a divorce. Three days later, Harvey married May Leake, formerly of Exeter, Missouri; she was 61 and he 78. She had come to Monte Ne in 1905, and by 1910, she was cooking at some of the Monte Ne hotels. In April 1920, Leake became Harvey's private secretary. From that point on, the local newspapers reported on the two from time to time, taking trips or working together. The marriage was performed at the Harvey home (seen here about 1930), and when asked by reporters if a honeymoon would be taken, Harvey replied, "The honeymoon shines brightest at home." About a week later, the community shivareed the Harveys by throwing a noisy mock serenade for the newlyweds. (Courtesy of the Arizona Historical Society/Tucson #6463.)

The stock market crash in the fall of 1929 ended all work on the Pyramid. But Harvey had been working on what he considered "the most valuable book I have ever written," and he published it in early 1930. *The Book* dealt with the harmful effects of usury by the government, calling money lending "destructive to the organism of the government and the life of this civilization." (Courtesy of RHM.)

THE BUGLE CALL

CALLING THE PEOPLE TO THE DEFENSE OF THE NATION AT THE BALLOT BOX

VOL. 1, NO. 1, MAY NUMBER, 1931 — ROGERS, ARKANSAS — SUBSCRIPTION 25 CENTS A YEAR

THE BUGLE CALL

Calling The People To The Defense Of The Nation At The Ballot Box

The Mundus Publishing Company, Publishers

Rogers, Arkansas, Route 1, Pyramid Box

W. H. (COIN) HARVEY, Editor.

Application for second class privilege applied for.

THIS IS THE FIRST number of a monthly, four page paper that may be, later, enlarged. The time has arrived when it is vitally necessary that such a paper should be published with news of the progress and growth of this Educational and Political movement. It is to be hoped that we can give this paper, in the near future, a circulation of more than a million copies. With the hundreds already helping a good start should be quickly made.

It is not only necessary that this paper, in quantity lots, should go to those who are assisting, but through them, to the tens of thousands who do not yet know of this movement or the cause of present disorder in the World; and to those who may be awakened from their apathy and indifference to realize that they are threatened with slavery to a heartless and merciless plutocracy of wealth; who will then become as anxious and unselfish as we are to promote this cause on which depends the life of free government and the happiness and prosperity of the human race.

To facilitate the rapid circulation of this paper to get the TRUTH to the people, we are fixing the following low prices for it:

One annual subscription 25 cents. Five copies to one subscriber one dollar.

To secure bundles of any one issue of 10 or more, it will be one cent per copy, ten copies for 10 cents, 100 for $1.00, 500 for $5.00.

Prices for this paper and "The Book" going to Canada, add 20 per cent.

The replies to our circular letter asking for subscriptions and orders in quantity lots is very gratifying. A few have misunderstood the difference in price of five papers, annually, to one person and five to five separate names; in the latter instance it is 25c each. Only five for $1.00 when all is going to one person, if the five go seperately to five names it is $1.25. It costs us about 5c per name entered on our books and set in type, the metal tied up for one year, this with bookkeeping and incidental expense cost us the difference between five copies for $1.00 and five copies to five names.

We do not expect to take any advertising, so there will be no revenue from that source, the paper must be financed on receipts from subscriptions and sales in quantity lots.

AN EVIL GIANT of destructive force is stalking through the nations of the world treading under foot the liberties and happiness of the human race—with the power to suppress the truth. Hence the importance of this journal, with a circulation that goes to millions of people.

The monster Evil with which we contend, has monopolized the money with which it gets its evil power, making it difficult for the people to finance the expense necessary in getting the truth to the people. But all can help a little and each $1.00 contributed to the circulation of this paper is next in importance to buying necessities such as food and clothing.

This is a Crusade on which life, liberty and human happiness depends—and in the future ability to buy food and clothing. Realizing the importance of it we are asking one and all, to buy, at one cent per copy, The Bugle Call, as many as they can and distribute them among the people. It is to be hoped that it will be millions of copies.

We are first running 20,000 copies of this issue; and the page forms will be put back on the press for more runs as the demand calls for them.

UNITED WE WIN

UNDER A MONSTROUS and iniquitous financial system the country has been bonded and mortgaged for interest bearing debts amounting to 150 billion dollars, more than the fair cash value of all assessable property in the United States, drawing an annual interest of Nine billion dollars, more than all the money in the nation; that is confiscating by foreclosure the property of the industrious people; and transferring the wealth of the nation to the money lenders who, as a rule, do not make a blade of grass grow.

This frightful condition is creating general bankruptcy, the farmers losing their homes, the business men their business, millions of unemployed, the breaking down of the organism of government with fear and anxiety among all the people, rich and poor, as to what the coming result will be.

The Monopolies, Trusts and Combines are united to enforce this present wicked system—have the two old political parties under their control—and are but waiting for the opportunity that will be created by the rising increase in bankruptcies, bank failures, non payment of taxes, the breaking down of the organism of government, the crime wave, rioting and confusion that will warrant them in risking the approval of the people in taking the dread step, a dictatorship, despotism, that will be the end of free government with a bloody civil war in this land.

Free speech, free press, the right of the people to peaceably assemble to discuss a remedy, will be gone under a dictatorship as it is now in Italy with liberty loving men imprisoned on the rocky islands in the Mediterranean.

The issue in the next election should be the saving of free government as against dictatorship and despotism. All differences of opinion should be laid aside until a free government is firmly established with honest men of wisdom in control of the government. Reformers can all unite on abolishing the present wicked financial system, the government ownership of the banking system, a moratorium law suspending for a time fixed, the collection of all interest bearing bonds and mortgages, till statesmanlike wisdom decides what is to be done with these debts. The only relief is for the people to unite in one New Political Party. United we will win!

The cause of present world distress must get to the people; and all to whom the Truth is revealed will unite with us. The Truth is being suppressed by the press, owned or under control of the money power. Nearly all the people now living are uninformed as to the cause of world distress, and do not know the fate of all countries that have been ruled by dictatorship. And the same fate will come to this country under dictatorship that came to the Roman Republic when it was overthrown and came under the rule of dictators.

We here quote from history the result of dictatorship in Rome, the fate that will come to all nations thus ruled.

> "Cities were sacked, fortresses leveled, churches burned, monasteries of both sexes destroyed, the fields wasted and the country abandoned so that wild beasts supplied the place of men. (Europe in the Middle Ages, by Dunham, Vol. I, Page 229.)

With untold millions suffering, the responsibility is great of those who are fostering, aiding and abetting this crime within the law.

This monster Evil Power has drawn to its assistance thousands of people of limited means, who are investing in bonds, small loans on mortgages and drawing interest on saving deposits in the banks; and the interest they are getting selfishly blinds them to support the system, that will eventually take from them all their wealth, unmindful in the meantime of the coming destruction, that the Usury system will bring if permitted to continue, when "Cities" will "be sacked, fortresses leveled, churches burned, monasteries of both sexes destroyed, the fields wasted and the country abandoned so that wild beasts will 'supply the place of men.'"

To the millionaires and billionaires who are profiting by this wicked system we would appeal to them to consider the fate coming to them and their descendants who will be engulfed in the maelstrom of coming destruction.

We have published a book entitled The Book that makes this subject as plain as 2 and 2 is 4. The price of it is 25c. No one should be satisfied or dismiss this subject till he has read it.

Believing his economic theories were affirmed by the stock market crash and ensuing Depression, Harvey once again turned to politics to advance his ideas. In 1930, he formed the Liberty Party, whose only platform was a revision of the country's monetary system. That May, he began publishing a newsletter, the *Bugle Call*, which championed the Liberty Party and *The Book* and called delegates to an upcoming convention. (Courtesy of RHM.)

After visiting other Midwestern locations, Harvey and the national Liberty Party committee decided to hold their convention at Monte Ne, the only presidential convention ever held in Arkansas. Harvey prepared with railroad excursion rates, media facilities, upgraded roads, and food concessions, anticipating 10,000 delegates. He tented the amphitheater, set up seating (top), and installed an amplifier system to reach the thousands to be seated outside. Delegates (bottom, with Harvey, seated) were only eligible to attend if they certified they had read and agreed with the principles of *The Book*. In the end, only 786 delegates attended, and Harvey was the only candidate the delegates could agree upon. They nominated Andrae Nordskog of Los Angeles for vice-president. (Courtesy of AP/Wide World Photos.)

Section 435 1-2 P. L. R.
U. S. POSTAGE
1c PAID
Rogers, Arkansas
PERMIT NO. 30

The Liberty Bell

Announcing A Second Declaration of Independence

C. W. HENNINGER Editor

1 Cent Per Copy for Extra Copies of This Paper

Published Monthly by The Mundus Publishing Co., Monte Ne, Arkansas

"The Book" single copy 25c; 6 for $1.00 "A Tale of Two Nations" single copy 30c; 4 for $1.00

VOLUME—1 December Number, 1931 NUMBER—1

THE LIBERTY BELL

We deem it essential that a printed Journal should go from the National Office, monthly. To cover the expense, we make it a subscription price of 50 cents per year. All names thus coming in will be enrolled in our office, and, will get it monthly. We would like to have 1,000 subscribers in the next 20 days.

FOR PRESIDENT

WILLIAM HOPE HARVEY of Arkansas

FOR VICE PRESIDENT

ANDRAE B. NORDSKOG of California

C. W. HENNINGER, Chairman of the National Committee

C. G. EVANS, Secretary

NATIONAL COMMITTEE

C. W. Henninger, Monte Ne, Ark.
H. A. Entrekin, Birmingham, Ala.
M. V. Hartranft, Los Angeles, Calif.
L. R. Tillman, Glenville, Ga.
Volney Sellers, Barry, Ill.
Forrest L. Hackley, Indianapolis, Ind.
Dr. Chas. Morrison, Coffeyville, Kans.
Joseph W. Hannan, Worcester, Mass.
Dr. G. D. Ball, Addison, Mich.
Chas. Perrine, Hollandale, Minn.
Tolley Hartwick, Miles City, Mont.
Homer Earl, Lincoln, Nebr.
Dr. C. C. Hibbs, Bismark, N. Dak.
Judge Chas. Bonsall, Salem, Ohio
John G. Zook, Lititz, Penna.
Howard Platt, Langford, S. Dak.
Dr. P. A. Spain, Paris, Texas

We are not certain this is all as Mr. Jackson took the list away with him. More will be added in time till all the states are represented.

All communications should be addressed to C. W. Henninger, Chairman, or C. G. Evans, Secretary, or to Mr. Harvey, whose home is here.

THE COMMITTEE

THE RULE governing each member of the National Committee is that it becomes his duty to promote the principles of the Platform and the election of the Candidates nominated by the Convention.

If a member of the Committee violates this rule and principle by seeking to prejudice people against the candidates nominated by the convention; or by direction or indirection trying to defeat the principles contained in the platform; such a Committeeman automatically, by his own act, eliminates himself as a member of the committee. And the right of anyone to officially recognize him as a member of the Committee has ceased.

If at a meeting of our National Committee, a majority present, and the meeting, legally called with opportunity for all to be present; and a competent Chairman presiding; a motion or resolution was offered recommending that their Candidate for President or Vice President be requested to resign; the Chairman would declare it out of order, as beyond the province of the National Committee and would reprimand the Committeeman making such a motion or offering such a resolution.

The three members of the Committee who met at Tulsa, taking the action they did have eliminated themselves from the National Committee. Mr. Bruner has voluntarily resigned as a member of the Committee, and, the other two have by their acts resigned. And their names are dropped from the roll of the Committee.

The Allie Reed meeting at Omaha had 11 persons present, 7 of them from Omaha. It was a failure.

Reorganization of the National Committee

WHAT HAS OCCURED SINCE ADJOURNMENT OF THE NATIONAL CONVENTION ORGANIZING THE LIBERTY PARTY

WITH A STARTLING CLIMAX THAT IS BRINGING US TENS OF THOUSANDS OF FRIENDS

IMMEDIATELY following the adjournment of the Convention the National Committee, one representing each of the sixteen states, met and Mr. James G. Jackson of Indiana was made Chairman. It was decided that National headquarters would be at Monte Ne, where Mr. Harvey the candidate for President lives and where he has a spacious office. An office building was built for Mr. Jackson located close to Mr. Harvey's office.

Last Christmas, nearly a year ago, a book appeared, entitled "The Book", written by Mr. Harvey, giving in a clear and convincing manner the cause of the present situation in the world and the Remedy. It was by the author of "Coin's Financial School" and "A Tale of Two Nations", the two having had a paid circulation of two million copies in 1894, 1895 and 1896, awakening the nation to the importance of the financial subject resulting in the nomination of Mr. Bryan for President in 1896, defeated by the money power with the use of money.

"The Book" by the same author attracted quick attention, beginning its paid circulation in January of this year. It dealt with the money subject, its history since the birth of this civilization, bringing it up to date, and went rapidly into circulation. By August it was circulating by copies going into every state in the union and orders for it coming in, in lots of 100 and 1,000. The awakening that came with its circulation brought together the convention that met at Monte Ne, August 25th of this year.

The convention, notwithstanding his request not to do so, nominated Mr. Harvey as the candidate for The Liberty Party for President of the United States.

Mr. Harvey, with forty years experience in education and organization, immediately began, following the adjournment of the Convention, put his office at work continuing the promotion of the sale of "The Book" and the work of organizing the Liberty Party. But depending for aid on the National Committee, first Mr. Jackson and secondly each member of the National Committee in their respective states, with more members of the National Committee, to follow in the other states.

And, now, we are going to let Mr. Harvey tell the story of what followed that has ended in trouble and confusion and the re-organization of the National Committee.

REORGANIZATION

By W. H. Harvey

Mr. Jackson took charge of his office September 12th. To get him acquainted with information from my office where a flood of letters, and orders for "The Book", were coming daily, I had him read these letters, sit and listen to the reading of the letters as they were read to me, till he saw that here in my office were the names of hundreds of men and women with whom he should get in touch, and in their respective states put members of the National Committee in touch with these people the numbers of them increasing daily through letters to my office, furnishing a splendid foundation for building up organization.

I soon found that Mr. Jackson was inactive doing nothing that was expected of him, with Mr. J. M. Smith, a member of the Committee for Arkansas and three or four other men living at Rogers, where Mr. Smith lives, coming and going from Mr. Jackson's office, not communicating to me what they were discussing, except that Jackson had made Mr. Smith his Secretary. No other members of the National Committee came here during Mr. Jackson's residence here. He and the men I refer to did discuss with me how money was to be raised, they claiming that nothing could be done until money was raised. I was pushing the work from my office at a nominal expense, taking care of postage and a small office force with a very small amount coming in from contributions, and I was setting people at work selling books and organizing in many states and I suggested that Mr. Jackson, Mr. Smith and these men coming to his office, with a nominal amount of money could do work the same way that I was doing it. But what I said did not seem to satisfy them.

I have since learned that the result of their many conferences in Mr. Jackson's office was that money could not be raised in sufficient amount without getting it from rich men and that that could not be done till they got rid of me as the candidate for President on the Liberty Party ticket. That these rich men were connected with banking, money lending, monopolies and combinations who were in favor of the present financial system and would not contribute to the Campaign Fund of the Liberty Party with me as its candidate.

On October 12th Mr. Jackson left here for Indiana, leaving instructions at the Post Office for all mail addressed to the Liberty Party, to the National Committee or to him as its Chairman to be delivered to Mr. J. M. Smith at Rogers, and any personal mail for him to be forwarded to Dublin, Indiana. Excepting two letters containing orders for The Book I have seen none of this mail, it all going to Mr. Smith at Rogers who has refused to let me see and has declined to instruct the Postmaster to deliver any of these letters to me.

On October 26th I received a Telegram from Mr. M. V. Hartranft of Los Angeles, a member of the National Committee that he "could not be present at the Tulsa meeting". This was the first I heard that there was to be such a meeting; and on inquiry of Mr. Smith learned that he had called such a meeting, to discuss the retirement of Mr. Jackson as Chairman, who should take his place and to confer with a wealthy man in Tulsa from whom they believed they could get a contribution to the Campaign Fund. He promised me that nothing would be done and no conclusion reached, decided on, till the meeting adjourned to meet with me the following day.

The next thing I learned was that the meeting here, instead of the following day, would be on Tuesday, November the third. What followed on November the third I gave to the press and it here follows:

HERE IS THE STORY

"A recent meeting was held at Tulsa, called without my knowledge, by Mr. Jackson's Secretary, at which eight men were present among whom were three members of the National Committee. The result of this meeting was communicated to me by E. M. Clark and W. H. Lyon of Rogers, Ark., D. H. Lauderback of Springdale, Ark., and George Moody of Tulsa, four of the eight who took part in this meeting. They said they represented all who took part in the meeting to report to me the result. That they, all the eight, recommended that we accept a proposition made them by a millionaire oil man, whose name was given me, that I resign as nominee for President, consent to Senator Norris of Nebraska taking my place and I support Norris, that he, this oil man, would pay down, cash, Twenty-five thousand dollars, and, in thirty days one million dollars into our Campaign Fund.

"The four men coming to me said the eight recom-

(Continued on next page)

There were rifts in the Liberty Party, however. Harvey turned down an offer of $1 million to the party and $25,000 to Harvey from a Tulsa millionaire for his resignation and support of another candidate. And Harvey demanded the resignation of Nordskog after he began charging for his political speeches. In April 1932, the Liberty Party merged with the Jobless Party under Fr. James R. Cox, but both Harvey and Cox ran independently for president. Harvey began the monthly publication of the Liberty Party's newspaper, the *Liberty Bell*, in December 1931. In the November 1932 election, Franklin Roosevelt won the presidency. Harvey came in fifth with 53,425 votes, mostly from the Western mining states. He received only two votes in Rogers and failed to carry Benton County. (Courtesy of RHM.)

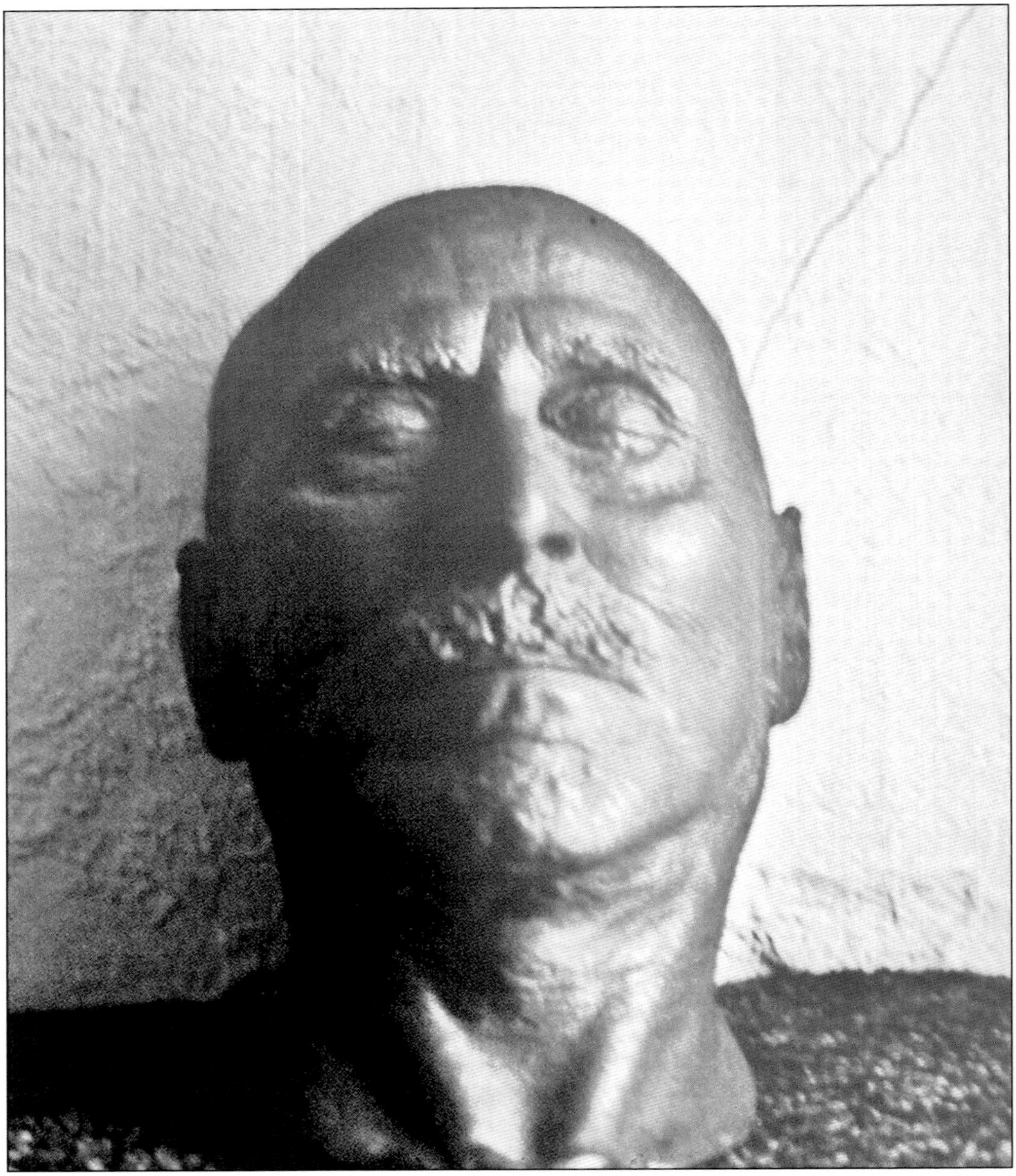

After the 1932 election, Harvey continued to publish the *Liberty Bell* (through June 1935) and to sell copies of his books, especially *The Book*. He remained steadfast in his opinions about usury, free silver, and the failure of the American economic system. In 1935, he blasted President Roosevelt's silver-buying policy (calling it a travesty) and his gold-buying program (calling it unconstitutional). His health remained a problem, and his eyesight failed altogether. On February 11, 1936, Harvey died at his home in Monte Ne due to peritonitis after an attack of intestinal influenza. His wife, May, was at his bedside, and son Tom arrived the next day; daughters Hope and Annette reportedly were too ill to travel. While his body lay at Callison's Funeral Home in Rogers awaiting preparation of his tomb, employee Ortis McKinney made a death mask of the 84-year-old Harvey, which is now in the collection of the Rogers Historical Museum in Rogers, Arkansas. (Courtesy of RHM.)

The tomb that had been built in 1903 to house the remains of Harvey's son Hal (Robert Halliday Harvey) was blasted open for the new burial. Between Harvey's casket—a simple, cheap pine box—and that of his son was placed a glass casket that had been obtained from Fort Smith and filled with two copies of Harvey's books and some of his other papers. The tomb was then resealed. A small funeral was held on February 14, 1936, with a log fire to keep the attendees warm. Rogers attorney W. B. Holyfield gave the eulogy. A single bronze plaque bearing the names and dates of the two Harvey men was posted. (Courtesy of RHM.)

Harvey died without a will, with a cash balance of $158, and owing $3,000. The Pyramid Association, however, which Harvey had created in 1929 from the dissolved Monte Ne Investment Company, still included 330 acres of land. In 1939, the courts ruled that all of Harvey's assets belonged to his wife, May, and between 1939 and 1948, she sold the last of the land and water rights to the old Monte Ne resort. Most of the land went to Chicagoan W. R. Feemster, with his brother, Cecil of Rogers, assisting with the deal. By 1941, May Harvey had left Monte Ne for Springfield, Missouri, and it is doubtful she ever returned before her death in October 1948 at her brother's home in Exeter, Missouri. (Courtesy of SMOH/Washington County Historical Society.)

Nine

Monte Ne after "Coin" Harvey

By the 1940s, the once-splendid hotels, gondola rides, Monte Ne railroad, and dances were all things of the past. In April 1944, both Missouri and Oklahoma Row (the Club House Hotel) were sold to Roy Joyce and Jim Barrack, Springdale businessmen. Missouri Row, more than 38 years old, was to be torn down and sold in small lots. The roof tiles were bought almost immediately by a Little Rock firm. By 1956, the *Daily Oklahoman* reported that the building had "collapsed into rubble," leaving only a small section standing. (Courtesy of RHM.)

In November 1944, D. L. King of Rogers bought the Monte Ne bank block (top), which he remodeled and made home to his Atlas Manufacturing Company, producers of poultry equipment. The company moved back to Rogers in March 1945. The building then stood idle for all of its remaining years, the window sashes and panes long ago having been broken or stolen and the walls later home to graffiti and vandalism (bottom). (Top courtesy of SMOH/Howard Clark; bottom courtesy of James Maxwell Skipper.)

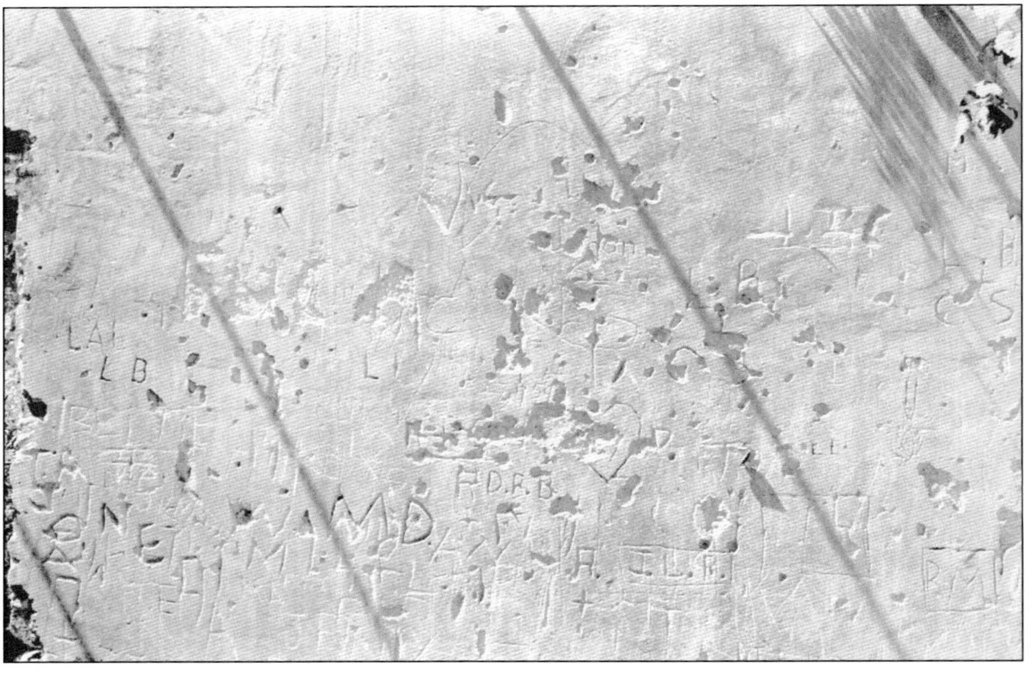

In the 1930s and 1940s, Oklahoma Row (the Club House Hotel) continued to provide lodging, although it was run and managed by a number of different people. In June 1946, Company G of the Arkansas State Guard held camp at Monte Ne for field training, using some of the hotel facilities. Access to Monte Ne improved a bit in August 1947 when the state highway department blacktopped 1.4 miles of the Monte Ne road. But it was clear that times had changed; in January 1948, six Monte Ne men were arrested for grand larceny, charged with stealing doors from the Club House Hotel and 500 feet of pipe from the swimming pool. (Top courtesy of RHM/Betty Swearingen; bottom courtesy of RHM.)

In July 1945, Iris Armstrong, owner of Camp Joyzelle, a girls' camp established just southeast of the amphitheater in 1923, used Oklahoma Row for camp activities and especially as lodging for people coming to visit the campers. Up until 1962, the Joyzelle girls held social events and activities such as plays and campfire ceremonies at the amphitheater (top, in 1959). Harvey said he didn't like children, but he could often be found in his later days sitting in the amphitheater watching the camp performances. The camp also used the ticketing section of the old railroad depot (bottom) for its main lodge and crafts building. (Top courtesy of RHM/Paula Thompson; bottom courtesy of SMOH/Washington County Historical Society.)

Other activities went on in Monte Ne following Harvey's death. In March 1946, a Baptist church was organized at Monte Ne under the sponsorship of the Benton County Baptist Association as a result of a series of revival meetings conducted there. The Monte Ne Baptist Church is still an active church today. For a time in the summer of 1946, the Rogers Intermediate Girl Scouts held a camp at the Hotel Frances (the old Hotel Monte Ne). Although it wasn't as active as it once was, the old filling station and Hummel store, then run by the Grahams in downtown Monte Ne and pictured here in the 1950s, continued to serve the local population as well as delight sugar-hungry campers from Joyzelle. David Myers opened the Monte Ne Inn, home to the "best fried chicken in Northwest Arkansas," in 1972 and continues to serve both area diners and visitors who come to see Coin Harvey's legacy. (Courtesy of RHM/Duane Hand.)

In 1948, Mr. and Mrs. W. T. McWhorter purchased from W. R. Feemster Coin Harvey's former log home and office (top) and the amphitheater. They moved into the house and in June 1949 opened it as an "elite eating place" called the Harvey House, specializing in steaks, chicken, and fish. Son Jim McWhorter ran the concession stand at the amphitheater (bottom) until about 1957. The stand sold Cokes, candy, souvenirs, and "The Story of 'Coin' Harvey," a pamphlet written by Mrs. McWhorter. (Top courtesy of SMOH/Washington County Historical Society; bottom courtesy of James Maxwell Skipper.)

In 1955, Dallas Barrack, a Springdale antique dealer, bought the Club House Hotel and renovated it into an antique store called the Palace Art Galleries (top). He carried some of the finest antiques in the area, and no doubt their setting in the historic and still grand rooms of the old Oklahoma Row (bottom) added value to their purchase. (Top courtesy of SMOH; bottom courtesy of SMOH/ Washington County Historical Society.)

By the 1950s and early 1960s, many people who visited Monte Ne, especially those coming to see the amphitheater, had no remembrance or knowledge of Coin Harvey, his resort, or his Pyramid project. The amphitheater, with its concrete construction and distinctive cement chairs, couches, and benches, was a striking spot for visitors to gather, picnic, and be photographed. (Courtesy of RHM.)

In January 1957, the *Tulsa Daily World* reported that 30,000 tourists visited Monte Ne annually "to look at [Harvey's] decaying testimonial." Not all visitors were tourists, however. The Arkansas State Historical Society held its 1960 annual meeting at Monte Ne (top) and gathered at the amphitheater to hear Clara Kennan (bottom) give a talk on Harvey and his Pyramid project. Kennan was born and raised in Rogers, Arkansas, taught school for more than 30 years, and was fascinated by Monte Ne her entire life. Her research and oral history interviews provide some of the best information on the story of Coin Harvey and Monte Ne. (Courtesy of SMOH/Benton County Historical Society.)

The amphitheater at Monte Ne was born of Harvey's frustration with the government's economic system, his desire to leave for the future a record of the early 20th century, and his passion for the use of concrete as a building material. Despite that serious and sobering birth, the amphitheater has continued to interest people of all walks of life who have delighted in visiting the site and, sometimes, simply playing there. (Courtesy of SMOH/Howard Clark.)

Ten

The Coming of Beaver Lake

Discussion of damming the White River for flood control began in the 1930s, and the U.S. Army Corps of Engineers (COE) held hearings on building a dam in January 1946. The dam would create a lake 50 miles long, and one arm would extend to Monte Ne. Work on Beaver Dam began in 1960 as the COE impounded and bought land around the White River. In July 1962, Mary Powell sold Camp Joyzelle to the COE, and W. T. McWhorter sold his land also. The dam was completed and Beaver Lake was at full height by June 1966. (Courtesy of RHM.)

In preparation for the flooding, the COE relocated cemeteries throughout the White River valley. The same fate awaited the Harvey tomb in 1962. Under contractor Harold Mathis of Springdale, the job took 10 days—nine simply to raise the 40-ton tomb and one to move it. The task, however, was not easy. The first attempt broke the bed of a flatbed truck. Loading the tomb bent the steel skids, which had to be reinforced. Then the Mathis truck was not strong enough; a Huntsville contractor with an old army truck had to be called in. A new road was laid to the site where the tomb was to be placed, on land donated by Harvey's longtime friends Mr. and Mrs. Kenneth Doescher. (Courtesy of SMOH/Howard Clark.)

Today the tomb of Coin Harvey and his son, Hal, rests on private property visible from the Monte Ne boat launch on Beaver Lake. Relocation of the tomb undoubtedly put pressure on it, causing it to crack with age. Nonetheless, it is fitting that Harvey's tomb faces directly across the lake to the amphitheater, whenever it arises out of the water. Harvey surely would have liked that. (Courtesy of the author.)

The COE's 1955 land survey mistakenly calculated that the waters of Beaver Lake would cover the area of the large hotels, so those parcels were added to the land they purchased for the project. Dallas Barrack, who owned Oklahoma Row, like many landowners around the White River valley, felt that he was treated poorly and received much less than his property was worth. The COE then held a sealed-bid auction, and J. G. Gladdens purchased the remainder of Missouri Row not already torn down or sold, as well as the Club House Hotel. He cleaned up the Missouri Row debris and planned to move the Club House Hotel out of the path of the rising lake waters. In order to do this, it was first necessary to remove the log portion or shell of the hotel (top). The original windows and doors were dismantled for the move and later reinstalled. The fireplaces, as well as all the major stonework (bottom), were later torn down. (Top courtesy of James Maxwell Skipper; bottom courtesy of SMOH/Howard Clark.)

A log portion of the original Oklahoma Row was moved north and now sits on the east side of Highway 94 in Monte Ne. It is used for storage, as seen here in 1998. Some of the original logs can still be seen, as can the red tile roof. (Courtesy of the author.)

Once the fireplaces and stonework were removed from Oklahoma Row and the log portion moved, the three-story concrete-and-stone tower (sometimes now referred to, erroneously, as the "honeymoon tower") showed evidence of where the stairway to the second story had been, as seen here in 1968. (Courtesy of James Maxwell Skipper.)

To the north of the Oklahoma Row tower lies the building's foundation minus its log portion, seen here in 1968. A careful look at the foundation will show missing inlay in the floor, which helps define each hotel room. Remains of the concrete fireplaces, chimneys, and other architectural elements are scattered around the foundation. (Courtesy of James Maxwell Skipper.)

Beneath the Oklahoma Row foundation on the northwest end lies the building's basement, its window and door sashes missing. During most of the year, the basement is under the waters of Beaver Lake. Only during period of drought is this section visible. (Courtesy of the author.)

On the northernmost end of the Oklahoma Row basement, there is a single hotel room, likely used for seasonal housekeeping staff and not for guests. Despite the effects of flooding and vandalism, the room can still be imagined in its original form, with its vaulted ceiling and fireplace (top) and bathroom facilities at the rear. Despite rumors to the contrary, the other rooms of the basement are simply well-constructed storage rooms (bottom). With their columns, archways, and inlaid floors, they were fancy storerooms for the oversize trunks that early-20th-century travelers usually brought with them on the train. Other effects kept in storage no doubt included hotel furniture, kitchen items, towels and linens, and perhaps food. (Courtesy of SMOH/*Springdale News* collection.)

The Oklahoma Row tower, viewed today across Beaver Lake from the amphitheater (top), may look like a beautiful building. On closer inspection, both inside and out, the tower suffers from neglect and vandalism, its walls and fireplaces spray-painted with graffiti (bottom), its stonework and concrete chipped, and its open spaces littered with trash. Although the hotel site was added to the National Register of Historic Sites in 1992, its status may be in peril, given its current state of disrepair. (Top courtesy of James Maxwell Skipper; bottom courtesy of the author.)

For many years, a rumor had surrounded the amphitheater. Having some idea that Harvey was to put items—perhaps valuable items—in the Pyramid, people assumed that those items must have been hidden in the amphitheater. Some believed there was a car there; others believed it was simply treasure. In 1963, one day before W. T. McWhorter was to transfer title of the Harvey home and Pyramid site to the COE, he was determined to dynamite the amphitheater to see if the rumored stash was really there. At the appointed time, a number of people showed up to see the explosion, but COE attorney David Waid arrived just in time to stop the detonation. Kenneth Doescher, who had worked as Harvey's secretary, heard many people claim the treasure was there, but he said he knew better. "I walked down there [by the amphitheater as it was being built] nearly every morning before breakfast," he said, and he believed that he certainly would have known had any treasure been placed inside. (Courtesy of James Maxwell Skipper.)

Beaver Lake started filling in January 1964, and power production began in May 1965. By that October, the lake had not yet covered Monte Ne, but it was slowly rising. As the lake waters approached, many took the time to visit and see, perhaps for the last time, some of the resort and Pyramid project of Coin Harvey. In the winter of 1963, many people paid a winter visit to Monte Ne (top). The bridge with embattlements (bottom), like other low-lying structures, was eventually covered by Beaver Lake (seen here in 1977 when the lake level dropped). (Top courtesy of RHM; bottom courtesy of RHM/Don Roemer.)

Ulis and Jerry Rose, then operators of the Town and Country Motel in Rogers, put in a sealed bid for the couch and chairs from the amphitheater stage. They acquired the chairs, which for a time sat outside their motel, but the couch was too heavy to move and still resides beneath Beaver Lake. The chairs were moved to Rogers's Frisco Park in the 1990s. (Courtesy of RHM.)

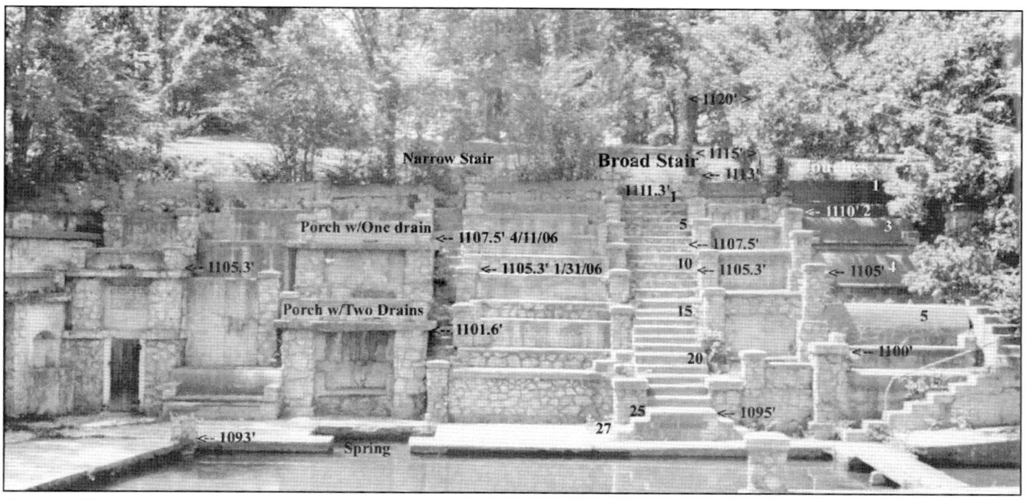

Beaver Dam maintains an average elevation of 1,120 feet above sea level, which, as seen here, is well above the top level of the amphitheater. In the late fall and early winter, it is not surprising for the very top of the structure to poke out of the water. However, during periods of great drought, all or a good part of the amphitheater can appear. (Courtesy of James Maxwell Skipper.)

With the lake level down several feet in the summer, here in the 1980s, a few rows of seating are revealed. Visitors found it an excellent place to swim. (Courtesy of RHM.)

The lake dropped to its lowest level on January 22, 1977, measuring 1,092.81 feet deep, or more than 27 feet below the lake's normal level. That winter, people came out in droves to see the amphitheater, both those who remembered it from bygone days and those who had never seen it. (Courtesy of RHM.)

Before Beaver Lake flooded downtown Monte Ne, the buildings were either moved or were bulldozed to avoid problems for swimmers, boaters, and anglers. The few bridges that spanned the lagoon were not demolished, but clearly they have suffered from being submerged for such a long time (top, in 1977). Scuba divers have long had an interest in diving by the amphitheater to get a good look at the structure (bottom). However, not only is the spring-fed water extremely cold, but it is also murky, resulting in little for a diver to see. Despite the fact that the amphitheater is underwater almost year-round, it was placed on the National Register of Historic Sites in 1978. (Top courtesy of RHM; bottom courtesy of SMOH/U.S. Army Corps of Engineers.)

Most people remember little about Missouri Row, since it was quietly torn down beginning in the 1940s. Today a Monte Ne visitor might not understand that it was once one of the proudest of resort buildings. A two-story, four-sided concrete fireplace from Missouri Row still stands on the site, surrounded by pieces of foundation, a few sets of stairs, some metal plumbing, and a small retaining wall. (Courtesy of the author.)

East of the Oklahoma Row tower and the Missouri Row fireplace, along the shoreline when Beaver Lake is very low, remnants of limestone structures can be seen. Some of these are foundations for the broad wooden staircase built in front of Hotel Monte Ne, some are structural components for the twin stone bridges that crossed the lagoon, and some are simply low retaining walls. (Courtesy of the author.)

Coin Harvey's life story is a fascinating tale combining elements of history, economics, politics, business, and tourism. He was clearly intelligent, entrepreneurial, hardworking, creative, and deeply rooted in his beliefs. Over the course of his lifetime, however, many people found him to be abrasive, egocentric, inflexible, ill-tempered, and miserly. His economic theories have in some cases stood the test of time, while his personality and quirkiness seemed always to work against him and his success at many life projects. Whether or not Harvey's contributions place him among the great individuals in American history, he certainly played a major role and contributed greatly to the history of Northwest Arkansas. (Courtesy of the Arizona Historical Society/Tucson #6462.)

A few remains of the glory that was once the Monte Ne resort are visible year-round: Harvey's tomb; the double fireplace of Missouri Row; the Oklahoma Row tower and foundation; the deteriorating log portion of Oklahoma Row on Highway 94; and the two concrete chairs from the amphitheater now in Rogers's Frisco Park. But when the waters of Beaver Lake recede, they present the gift of the Oklahoma Row basement, some of the limestone traces near the present-day boat launch, and,

most invitingly, the amphitheater itself. Although Harvey was not able to build the Pyramid, his monument that would explain the collapse of the 20th century, the amphitheater portion of his plan did get built and now continues as a reminder—whether underwater or exposed—of Coin Harvey and the story of historic Monte Ne. (Courtesy of James Maxwell Skipper.)

BIBLIOGRAPHY

Black, J. Dickson. *Coin Harvey and His Monte Ne*. Bentonville, AR: self-published, 1988.

Funk, Erwin. "The Day Monte Ne Saw Its First Railroad Train," *Benton County Pioneer* 3, 4 (May 1958): 10–14.

Harvey, W. H. "The Pyramid Booklet." Monte Ne, AR: The Pyramid Association, 1928.

Hughes, William Herschel. "Octogenarian Nominee of a Newborn Party." *Arkansas Historical Quarterly* 22 (Winter 1963): 291–300.

Kennan, Clara B. "The Ozark Trails and Arkansas's Pathfinder, Coin Harvey." *Arkansas Historical Quarterly* 7, 4 (Winter 1948): 299–316.

———. "Coin Harvey's Pyramid." *Arkansas Historical Quarterly* 6, 2 (Summer 1947): 132–144.

Lawler, Nan Marie. "The Ozarks Trails Association." M.A. thesis, University of Arkansas, 1991.

McWhorter, Mr. and Mrs. W. T. "The Story of 'Coin' Harvey." Monte Ne, AR: self-published, 1948.

Mitchell, Dorothy. "The Coin Harvey Saga." *The Ozarks Mountaineer* 18, 7 (August 1970): 18–21.

Nichols, Jeannette P. "Bryan's Benefactor: Coin Harvey and His World." *The Ohio Historical Quarterly* 67, 4 (October 1958): 299–325.

Randolph, Vance. "Coin Harvey." *The Ozarks Mountaineer* (May 1978): 22, 23, 27.

Riley, Robert. *Coin Harvey and Monte Ne*. Self-published, 1977.

Schick, Robert. "The Story of Coin Harvey." *Arkansas Gazette*. October 31, 1948: 1.

Snelling, Lois. *Coin Harvey, Prophet of Monte Ne*. Point Lookout, MO: School of the Ozarks, 1973.

William H. "Coin" Harvey and Monte Ne Collection. Research Library. Rogers Historical Museum, Rogers, Arkansas.

INDEX